The Trustee Governance Guide

"With this book, Merker and Peck put forth a highly useful guide for both board members and those with an interest in coaching boards to achieve better financial outcomes for their organizations. Their thoughtful and focused work lays out practical approaches for avoiding the myriad impediments, which can prevent successful governance and institutional investing. Their prescriptions are concise, interesting and actionable—this should be a must read for investment committee heads nationwide. Bravo."

—Sterling Shea, *Global Head of Wealth & Asset Management, Dow Jones*

"Everywhere we look, fiduciary duties, norms, standards, and processes continue to receive heightened scrutiny in the wake of the last financial crisis and the worldwide growth of socially responsible investing strategies. This book offers a timely, understandable, enlightening, and critically important discussion of the importance of fiduciaries to investment performance and the role of governance in driving fiduciary quality complete with useful tips and tactics for practitioners in finance."

—John Taft, *Vice Chairman, Baird*

"This book puts the 'G' in Environmental, Social and Governance factors for impact investing. ESG is not a trend, it is a mega trend—and for good reason. As Merker and Peck prove, an ESG approach to management and governance adds value to sponsors, participants and to society. It is incumbent upon fiduciaries to understand the implications and process behind this win/win/win approach to portfolio management. Thought provoking and full of compelling data, *The Trustee Governance Guide* is an approachable and actionable book for trustees and fiduciaries of any skill level to understand the potential benefits of sustainable investing and governance."

—Tom Anderson, *Former Executive Director of Morgan Stanley Wealth Management; Author of The Value of Debt series; Executive Chairman of Supernova Companies*

Christopher K. Merker • Sarah W. Peck

The Trustee Governance Guide

The Five Imperatives of 21st Century Investing

palgrave
macmillan

Christopher K. Merker
Fund Governance Analytics
Milwaukee, WI, USA

Sarah W. Peck
College of Business
Marquette University
Milwaukee, WI, USA

ISBN 978-3-030-21087-8   ISBN 978-3-030-21088-5   (eBook)
https://doi.org/10.1007/978-3-030-21088-5

This Palgrave Macmillan imprint is published by the registered company Springer Nature Switzerland AG
The registered company address is: Gewerbestrasse 11, 6330 Cham, Switzerland

Dedicated to our families.
From Chris to S, G, and K...you are the light and apples of my eye.
From Sarah to T, L, and M...you are my greatest joy.

Ten percent of proceeds from the sale of this book benefit the CFA Society Milwaukee Foundation and SecureFutures, partner organizations dedicated to fostering financial and investor literacy, locally and across the nation.

Foreword

Out of the 39 books on management practices Peter Drucker wrote during his long and illustrious career, only one dealt with pensions. He wrote *The Unseen Revolution* in 1976. In a reprint 20 years later, he would call it his "least-read but most prescient book". I was one of those few people who did read the book when it first came out in 1976. Through it, I saw how Drucker's pension revolution would unfold in the decades ahead, and decided to play a role in that unfolding.

In the book, he addressed three broad topics: (1) how the design and sponsorship of retirement income systems might unfold, (2) the issues around how these systems would be governed, and (3) how and in whose interests retirement savings would be invested. Forty-three years and four books later, I am still at it. Framing the pension revolution around integrating design, governance, and investing challenges was a stroke of Drucker genius. In one of the professional highlights of my life, I was able to tell him that in person in August 2005. At age 96, he died four months later.

Given Chris Merker and Sarah Peck's kind mention of my early work in trustee governance research in this book, I thought I should disclose the source of my original interest in the topic. To their credit, the authors too integrate governance issues into the effective fiduciary management of pension and endowment assets. Also to their credit, they do so in a reader-friendly manner. I fully appreciate the three reasons they give for 'why this book now': (1) governance as a process is finally receiving the bright spotlight it deserves, (2) the time has come to recognize the rise of behavioral economics and its lessons for trustee decision-making, and (3) sustainable investing is increasingly displacing "quarterly capitalism" as the philosophical foundation for long-term wealth creation. These three elements are neatly woven into their "five imperatives of 21st Century investing" for governing fiduciaries.

The authors deserve a special "shout-out" for the new research findings on the value of good governance they describe in the book. Using an extensive database on US public sector pension plans they themselves built over the course of the last few years, the authors make a significant contribution to the growing evidence that good governance is a value-creating 'asset' in itself. Specifically, using seven key drivers of governance quality to create a fiduciary effectiveness quotient (FEQ) for each fund in the database, they found that first quartile FEQ funds outperformed fifth quartile FEQ funds by a highly material average of 3.5% per annum.

I commend this book to all those with an interest in understanding what fiduciary effectiveness is, and have the aspiration to put it into practice.

International Centre for Pension Management   Keith Ambachtsheer
Rotman School of Management
University of Toronto
Toronto, ON, Canada

Preface

Since the 1990s, books on the topic of governance and investments seem to come around every few years. So, why is it time for another one? Well, a lot has changed in the past few years. First, there is the surge in ESG-oriented funds. ESG stands for environmental, social, and governance factors, which can be used in an investment process as a potential risk mitigation tool and can offer the prospect of promoting sustainable development goals. In the decade prior to 2015, ESG investing was largely a backwater, championed by only a socially conscious few. Now many boards are faced with figuring out how to align ESG or impact objectives with their fiduciary obligations to beneficiaries.

A 2017 study by McKinsey & Co. found that over a quarter of the $88 trillion of assets under management globally are now invested according to environmental, social, and governance principles.[1] And yet, while asset managers have jumped onboard the ESG movement, board trustees have been left trying to play catchup. A 2017 State Street survey of institutional investors captures one of the causes of the disconnect: 56% of ESG adopters indicated there is a lack of clarity over ESG terminology, along with confusion over what ESG is or should be.[2] The industry's confusion has spilled over to trustees, making their problem of how to address ESG even more intractable. We saw the need for a framework to help trustees to identify ESG goals and to integrate ESG into their investment policy. We provide that framework in this book.

---

[1] https://www.institutionalinvestor.com/article/b15cc1dxds8k97/mckinsey-esg-no-longer-niche-asassets-soar-globally

[2] https://www.ssga.com/investment-topics/environmental-social-governance/2018/04/esg-institutional-investor-survey.pdf

The second thing that has changed has been the focus of our research: the importance of how trustees govern *themselves* in achieving better financial outcomes. Industry and academia have long accepted the positive impact good *corporate* governance can have on stock and bond returns. While many boards have embraced the importance of corporate governance in making investments, they have struggled with how to govern themselves to achieve better returns for the assets entrusted to their care. Our research has sought to change that by taking an empirical approach to the problem—employing the same research paradigms used in the study of corporate governance.

While hard verifiable data on corporate governance is plentiful, there is no such data on trustee governance. The availability of good data has been a major obstacle to solid research on the topic of trustee governance. Before we began collecting data for our US public pension plans database, the data simply didn't exist. We assembled our initial database by hand collecting the information, lifting it from publicly available meeting minutes. That effort bore fruit. Through rigorous statistical analysis of our data, we established results that showed that trustee governance, like corporate governance, improves the financial outcomes of the plan's assets. More importantly, we were able to identify the board practices that matter. Through a series of articles and working papers, we began publishing our results. Then in 2018, we converted our method to a national survey. The next step was to make these findings available in book form to a much broader audience, hence this book.

Finally, the third change has been the acceptance of the role behavioral economics plays in investment decision-making. The behavioral economics movement began 40 years ago as an opposing theory to *homo economicus*, which has dominated our collective thinking since the Enlightenment. The "new" theory asserts that human beings apply heuristics to decision-making under a condition of either paucity of knowledge or too much information, leading to outcomes that are suboptimal. While this theory has been confirmed by study after study, the application to "real world" activity has been more limited. Trustees need to understand the pitfalls of their all too human behavior.

Research into—and better understanding of—best practices within the governance arena, how groups work together to drive more optimal outcomes especially within the context of investment management, we believe, offers one of the best opportunities to apply what has been learned from behavioral finance. Why? Quite simply because that is where the money is; 80% of financial assets in the US fall under the purview of an investment board.[3]

---

[3] "Proposed Rule: Definition of Fiduciary under ERISA", CFA Institute Letter to the Department of Labor, February 2, 2011.

If we want to drive better outcomes for investment decisions, we need to focus on the people who are responsible for them.

With any body of work, no one is an island, and for us we have many to thank over the course of this journey. First, we must thank our families for their love and support. To the many graduate assistants who have worked with us over the years, thank you for your contributions. At Marquette University, thank-you to the many of the faculty who supported us in this endeavor, particularly Farrohk Nourzad, especially on the econometric work, and Nadelle Grossman at Marquette Law, on corporate governance.

At Baird, thank-you to Michael Klein, head of the investment consulting group, Private Asset Management, and Duane McAllister, lead portfolio manager in the municipal bond area. We also thank Greg Allan and Anna West at Callan, who have been supportive of our work from very early on. Thank-you to Tula Weiss and Jacqui Young, our editors at Palgrave Macmillan. Lastly, our thanks to our friends and colleagues at Fund Governance Analytics: Bob Smith, Nicholas Erickson, Tony Baish, Dave Honan, Steve Vanourny, Dave Grosse, Tom Anderson, Mel Gill, Nathan Swanson, and Michael McMillan.

Milwaukee, WI, USA   Christopher K. Merker
December 21, 2018   Sarah W. Peck

Contents

List of Figures

List of Tables

1

Introduction

A fiduciary is anyone who is placed in a position of trust by another. Fiduciary duty is what has held civilization together since the beginning of human history. Our lives are better off for it, and we see examples of it everywhere we go: of the duty of parent to child, spouse to spouse, and often later in life, child to parent; doctor to patient, policymaker to constituent, manager to stockholder; and the list goes on. Trustees on an investment board also have a fiduciary duty to beneficiaries or donors. Like other types of fiduciaries, they are entrusted to act in others' interests, and not their own. Fiduciary duty is at the heart of this book.

Despite the long-term decline in defined benefit plans in American corporations, other retirement programs persist, including public and remaining corporate pension plans, managed and discretionary profit-sharing plans, and of course, the now ubiquitous 401(k), 403(b) or defined contribution plans. These programs continue to play a crucial role in providing retirement security and should be protected and sustained as much as possible. That responsibility lies within the fiduciary duty of the board of trustees overseeing these plans.

The field of investing is complicated, at times unnecessarily so, and most people are neither trained nor prepared for overseeing investments. Only a handful of states require some type of instruction as part of the basic educational curriculum for high schoolers.[1] Widespread financial illiteracy not only plagues our collective ability to invest as a society, but also hampers our ability to manage and maintain the basics of personal finance, including household

---

[1] https://www.ecs.org/high-school-graduation-requirements/

© The Author(s) 2019
C. K. Merker, S. W. Peck, *The Trustee Governance Guide*,
https://doi.org/10.1007/978-3-030-21088-5_1

budgeting and the responsible use of credit. This makes the role of the financial fiduciary even more critical to our economic health.

As a long-time practitioner in the field of investing, Chris has had the opportunity of working with many different clients over the years, and the chance to see the full range of activity and behaviors against a backdrop of a constantly shifting market environment.

About ten years ago, Chris began teaching what has now become "Sustainable Finance" in the Applied Investment Management (AIM) Program at Marquette University, taking over from Sarah, who originally designed the course, believed to be one of the first in the nation. The AIM program teaches select finance undergraduates applied training in investments. Graduates of the program go on to pursue careers in asset management, private equity, wealth management, and other roles across banking and finance. The focus of this course has been on ethics in the investment profession, but covers several other important topics, including corporate governance and socially responsible investing.

It has been said that the best way to become an expert in anything is to become a teacher of the subject. That was the case for Chris. Back when Chris was an MBA student, two decades ago, corporate governance was just coming into its own as a topic in MBA courses. So, when he began teaching it, he became a student all over again.

As he learned more about how the structure and organization of corporate boards could be empirically linked to organizational performance, he began reflecting on the many boards and committees he had worked with over the years with respect to their investments, and he wondered whether the different behaviors from these groups impacted their performance, and how this might change over time. In addition, he considered, with respect to his role as the investment consultant, to what degree his role was integral and influential in this process. Chris felt and had observed that these factors were important and seemed to impact the outcomes over time, but he didn't know how to go about answering these questions to any point of conclusiveness.

This led to our collaboration. Sarah is a corporate governance scholar who has spent her career developing methods for analyzing board governance factors, but also has practical experience in serving on a public pension plan board. Sarah, for seven years, chaired the Milwaukee County Public Pension Board investment committee. When Chris approached her on this topic, thinking it might make for an interesting Ph.D. research thesis, she immediately saw the potential for work in this area.

Between the two of us, we had a solid set of skills and experiences to identify and frame our research questions. Moreover, we were aware that the US public pension system was under siege. We hypothesized that if trustee governance mattered at all, it would matter most for organizations under stress. At the same time, we hoped, but did not know, that the results of our work could help, in albeit a small way, to alleviate the crisis.

The thing about exploratory research is, while you may have some ideas about the phenomenon you are looking into, you really don't know what you will find. In our case, we ended up finding some compelling evidence. And by the way, we shouldn't call this "new". There have been several others before us who have contributed their knowledge and findings to this area. Keith Ambachtsheer, a luminary in this field, was doing work back in the early 1990s. He was one of the first to see the importance of governance and did some of the initial survey work. Gordon Clark and Roger Urwin, in collaboration with Willis Towers Watson, have been systematic in their development of theory around this topic, and have been influential, particularly in working with industry on this. And there have been, of course, others whom we will also encounter at various points in this book.

Our goal in our work, and where we saw an opportunity to contribute, was in measuring the empirical relationship of governance factors to financial outcomes. The challenge was to gather data to do just that. But, we did it, and today we house the first and only public pension governance database, and we are working on expanding our work into other peer groups and related ESG areas.

So, why the **Five Imperatives**? First, what is an imperative? Webster's defines it as something that is "expressive of a command", an "obligatory act or duty",[2] as something that is "not to be avoided", but "necessary". For a board with great responsibility, nay, a *fiduciary-level* of responsibility to others whose livelihoods or missions depend on it, the use of the term "imperative" could not be more relevant.

Why focus on these five? In our view, most complexity can be broken down into a few digestible components. If we came to you and said we have 42 factors we want you to think about regarding your board governance (or even 144 factors, as one of our board evaluation instruments, the Governance Self-Assessment Checklist (GSAC), has the capacity to evaluate), your eyes would, no doubt, glaze over.

Instead, if we came to you and said, "There are five critical things that you, in running your organization's or even your own personal investment portfolio, must keep sight of", then we might have a different discussion.

---

[2] https://www.merriam-webster.com/dictionary/imperative

So, the goal of this book is to put our work and findings in the hands of the practitioner. In making this guidebook a *practical* guide, we have structured this book to address the five most critical areas facing every organization with an investment mandate. Each area has several subtopics related to it, which we will spend time with, but at the end of the day, and by the end of the book, we want this to be something that each trustee can take back to their boards and begin incorporating into regular practice and use to ultimately more effectively fulfill their fiduciary duty.

How to Use This Book

This book is divided into five sections, the Five Imperatives. Each section is further broken down into chapters that cover various topics under each imperative. We have also introduced within each section an investment subtopic, with a more technical emphasis geared toward the practitioner—a deeper dive into the mechanics of how to address a subject which relates to the overarching theme of the section. This book may be read cover to cover, or it can be picked at or used as a guide for later reference.

Our vision for how our work may impact the boards now and in the future is to help them to focus on the major drivers of positive change, and for us the big three are: **Governance**, through assessment and self-evaluation; **Performance (of** *both a financial and impact or "double-bottom line" nature***)**, through effective oversight and reporting; and finally, **Impact**, through proper evaluation and application of portfolio investments that drive better returns, mitigate risk, and home in on certain factors that better express the values and mission of the organization.

Part I

The First Imperative:
Be Well-Governed

2

Crisis

In August 2008, Chris appeared before a 15-member investment committee of a large trade association to explain the economics of the housing crisis. The committee was beginning to wrap its head, like many of us at the time, around the idea that a bubble had formed in housing and we were beginning to see cracks in the foundation of our financial system as a result. A few weeks later, of course, Lehman failed, and the rest is history. This organization later went on to liquidate a hefty portion of its investment portfolio in March 2009 to support unanticipated cash needs that arose because much of its membership and contributor base dried up. It, unfortunately, saw significant declines in the value of the portfolio, and raising cash from selling stock during a market decline came at a steep cost, as the portfolio never had the opportunity to recover in equity value along with the market in the months that followed. Today the organization is a shadow of its former self.

A corporate pension plan, around the same time, decided to liquidate at the direction of the trustees, fearing that the system was collapsing. That organization was left with two difficult decisions: when to exit the market and when to return. The return to the market did not come until much later. Again, this move was costly to the organization as fear overwhelmed investment discipline and is today at a funding status much lower than it would have been. It has been left to make up the difference with hundreds of thousands of dollars in additional annual contributions.

Sarah, in the meantime, saw the assets of the Milwaukee County Employees Retirement System take a dramatic plunge. The hole created by the financial crisis was filled in when the county issued a Pension Obligation Bond the following year. In subsequent years, the board made other changes to improve

© The Author(s) 2019
C. K. Merker, S. W. Peck, *The Trustee Governance Guide*,
https://doi.org/10.1007/978-3-030-21088-5_2

performance and be in a better position to weather the inevitable next market downturn.

Following the crisis, there was a rash of market-neutral funds and absolute return, so-called 130/30 funds, which are funds that allocate 30% of the fund into short positions, selling short stocks that are believed to be overvalued, and taking the proceeds and "going long" with the rest. The investment strategies claim to do well in any market environment, but the reality is that these strategies tend to do rather poorly, especially in a recovering equity market, and typically cost more. Infrastructure funds, fund of funds for hedge funds, and other types of investments purporting to provide higher returns with less risk were also pitched to boards.

Data from Mercer showed that while only around 4.5% of investments were in these fund types as compared to all global investment fund strategies earlier in the decade, this had tripled by 2009.[1] Using public pension plans' financial data from the Boston College Center for Retirement Research, we found that the use of alternative investments increased over 60% in the four years following the crisis. In behavioral finance, it is known as "backward looking" bias, a tendency for people and boards to increase (decrease) investments in asset classes that have recently performed well (poorly). Instead, boards should be forward-looking by asking, "Based on current valuations, what can each asset class reasonably expect to return on a forward basis"?

This repeated pattern of hedging market risk in equities after the 2008 decline was tantamount to putting on the brakes *after* going over a cliff. A tempting action to be sure, but far too late; the car had already crashed and was in flames. The best thing to do was to sit tight and wait for the flames to die out and for the car to get back on the road. Today, we've seen the reverse pattern as investors have piled into equities and reduced their alternative positions as alternatives have vastly underperformed equities over the following decade. In 2018, a record number of hedge funds closed for the third year in a row.[2]

Our initial study focused on the five years around the global financial crisis (GFC) period: the lead up, the crisis itself, the aftermath, and recovery. Chris began his doctoral work in 2011, and we began collecting data a year later for the years 2008–2012. As luck would have it, this created the opportunity to examine board governance under extreme conditions. The year 2008 was the second worst year in the markets over the past century, with only 1932 being

---

[1] Maton, Brendan, "Dissecting 'absolute return' methods", *Financial Times*, October 10, 2010. https://www.ft.com/content/a985b8a2-d307-11df-9ae9-00144feabdc0

[2] Kumar, Nishant and Waite, Suzy, "Hedge-Fund Closures Hit $3 Trillion Market as Veterans Surrender", Bloomberg, December, 13, 2018.

worse, when the world was in the grip of the Great Depression. We hypoth-esized that stronger forms of governance would win the day, and those orga-nizations would weather the storm better than those with weaker forms of governance. The alterative was that governance didn't matter at all to fund performance.

But before spending time painstakingly collecting governance data, we had to make sure there was enough return variation across plans to explain in the first place. We thought it was possible that public pension plans would likely make very similar investment decisions and thus have very similar returns. This, by the way, is every researcher's secret fear: that we would pull all the data and there would be no variation at all. In other words, nothing to study, and nothing to discern. Every organization would be and do as any other. The data from our sample from that time period (Fig. 2.1) certainly showed a high degree of variability.

That fear was entirely misplaced: lots of variation, lots of difference. Is this acceptable? If you as a consumer experienced that kind variation in perfor-mance from any other producer of goods and services, it is doubtful you would return for a second purchase. There is a reason why when you have breakfast at McDonald's, it doesn't matter if you have it in San Diego or Cleveland. It is virtually the same experience universally. To extend the anal-ogy and put it in comparable quantitative terms, it would be like sitting down

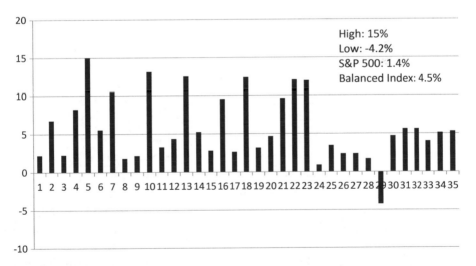

Fig. 2.1 US public pension funds' five-year average returns, 2008–2012. (Merker, Christopher Kinne, "Asset Owner Governance and Fiduciary Effectiveness: The Case of Public Pension Plans" (2017). *Dissertations (2009 -)*. 713, http://epublications.mar-quette.edu/dissertations_mu/713, p. 194)

on one side of the country and getting half a burger and sitting down on the other side of the country and receiving four burgers, all for the same price.

In the business of public retirement benefits production, the burgers are the returns trustees are earning on the funds to pay benefits. But taxpayers and employees who contribute to the fund must contribute either a lot or a little depending on the effectiveness of their fiduciaries. In a market-based system some variation in performance among service providers or manufacturers is acceptable within reason or regulatory requirements (i.e., airplanes are not allowed to crash, and children's toys are not permitted to be dangerous). Yet, when the system is not entirely market-based, then some other mechanism needs to come in to play for better, and more, consistent outcomes. That, based on our findings, is organizational governance.

Some did exceptionally well, but most, about 60%, did at or below the average. The top end of the scale was 15% annualized returns and the bottom, −4.5%. In dollar terms, there was a vast difference: approximately $1.6 billion per year on average. This surprised us because most funds share many of the same environmental factors, and by that we mean things like the demographics of the populations they serve, economic factors and budgetary constraints, political influences, and so on. So, what caused them to perform so differently?

We know, of course, that differences in asset allocations themselves can lead to performance differences. It is not rocket science to understand that more investments that do better drive higher returns versus those that do not. The timing or entry and exiting points into the asset classes or investments can be a driver as well. If you buy high and sell low, the performance, of course, will be diminished.

But what drives the investment choice? What triggers the entry or exiting decision? The board, often with the help of an investment consultant, ultimately makes these decisions. The review of facts and data, presentations by investment managers, the role of the staff or other outside experts, the trustees' discussion, the voting by trustees, all come together to bring about an investment choice. So, where does governance come into play?

Besides the impact on financial outcomes, governance also keeps the organization in line and conforming to norms, that is, no criminal acts, no self-dealing, no pay-to-play, and so on. We looked at that, too, and analyzed 2500 litigation cases over the five-year period to come up with a legal index of performance, and the first complete taxonomy of litigation case types in the public pension world, ranging from minor denial of benefits cases to Securities and Exchange Commission (SEC) cease and desist orders. As systems come under financial stress, the legal and regulatory system is often called upon to sort out the issues. In Chicago, the

Illinois Supreme Court twice struck down reduction in benefit requests submitted by the city mayor, Rahm Emmanuel. In the State of New Jersey, the SEC cited the legislature for improper disclosure of pension risk in municipal bond prospectuses. Only one of two times has this ever occurred at the state level, the other being in the state of Illinois.

For many years, the public pension system worked—it provided retirement benefits to government workers without placing undue burdens on taxpayers. The financial crisis in 2008, and for at least some plans, chronic underfunding along with the aging baby boomers has thrown the system into crisis. But so too have inconsistent and, at times, lax governance practices. Unlike the SEC regulation which stipulates governance practices for publicly held corporations, there are no such federal regulations for public pension plans. In this book we advocate boards voluntarily adopt evidence-based practices that can help mitigate the financial burden these plans create for taxpayers, perhaps help to alleviate some of the crisis, and get a number of systems back on track.

Warren Buffet once quipped that benign neglect, bordering on sloth, is the hallmark of his company's investment process. The wisdom and irony in that phrase is that Berkshire Hathaway is a very well-governed corporation. One might say on this basis: governance first and investing second.

3

Fiduciary Duty

Before we jump into a discussion about the characteristics of good board governance, it is important to review the onus placed on every board member: fiduciary duty. The discharged duty of the fiduciary may be considered the overarching exhortation that demands good governance. As the *Yale Law Journal* noted nearly 80 years ago, in the field of investing and its relation to the fiduciary:

> *Although the distinction between prudence and improvidence in the investment market is obscure, the trustee is obliged at his peril to discover that distinction.*[1]

The concept of fiduciary duty finds its sources in Roman law. The word "fiduciary" comes from the Latin *fiducia*, which refers to the transfer of a right to a person, who receives it, subject to an obligation to transfer it again at a future time or upon the fulfillment of a certain condition. This evokes the modern-day idea of a trust or of an asset held in escrow.[2]

Fiduciary duty represents a "cluster of obligations" owed by one person, the "trustee" or "fiduciary" toward another, the "cestui" or "beneficiary", regarding an identified subject matter, which is referred to as the "res" or "subject of the trust".

The conditions for a relationship that gives rise to a fiduciary duty is characterized by the following:

---

[1] https://www.jstor.org/stable/792579?seq=1#page_scan_tab_contents
[2] Chodos, 2000.

© The Author(s) 2019
C. K. Merker, S. W. Peck, *The Trustee Governance Guide*,
https://doi.org/10.1007/978-3-030-21088-5_3

- The duty has an **ambit,** meaning that it is owed toward a certain person or persons and not others.
- The duty has a **scope**, which means it entails certain obligations and not others.
- A duty may **terminate**, which means the engagement of the duty may end, but certain obligations may persist long after the termination date.
- A duty is either **discharged** or **breached**. In the case of a breach, the law may impose a **remedy**.

The duty can be either **asymmetrical** or **symmetrical** depending on the situation. A trustee of a pension plan owes a duty to the beneficiaries of the plan, but the beneficiaries owe her nothing. A husband and wife are fiduciaries for each other.

The "grammar" of fiduciary duty is essentially comprised of these four primary duties:

1. **Duty of Management or "Duty of Care"** This is most similar to a contracting duty, and it is the duty to do what has been undertaken to be done.
2. **Duty of Preference or "Duty of Trust"** This is the duty that is most similar to the original Roman concept, and it comes in two parts: (1) Duty of Preference is to set the interests of the *cestui* before one's own; (2) Duty of Loyalty is to set the interests of the *cestui* before all others (third parties).
3. **Duty to Account** The fiduciary must maintain records of all transactions affecting the *res* and provide a report of these transactions either on request or on a schedule. This means the fiduciary must not only be honest, but maintain the records proving she is honest.
4. **Duty of Disclosure** The final duty relates to the duty to account, but goes one step further. This duty requires the trustee to keep the *cestui* fully informed as to all facts, which are or might be pertinent to the *cestui's* interest in the trust. While the duty to account refers to transactions that have already taken place, the duty of disclosure refers to transactions that *may* take place in the future. These duties carry no direct benefit themselves other than to ensure the *cestui* is privy to all information, thereby enabling her to protect her rights.

We have come a long way from the days of the legal interpretation of the Prudent Man Rule. The Prudent Man Rule originated in the 1830 case *Harvard College v. Amory*, where the judge ruled that trustees were obligated "to observe how men of prudence, discretion and intelligence manage their own affairs, not in regard to speculation, but in regard to the permanent disposition of their funds, considering the probable income, as well as the probable safety of the capital to be invested".[3] Many states codified this rule by legally requiring trustees to list the securities that were permitted for purchase in the trust. The development of modern portfolio theory pushed the legal definition further. Codified in Employee Retirement Income Security Act of 1974 (ERISA)[4] for corporate pensions, and in the Uniform Prudent Management of Institutional Funds Act (UPMIFA) for endowments and foundations, institutional investors now have full latitude on over their investments. For certain types of investors there remain some restrictions. For example, in the state of Wisconsin, if you are a school district, unless you have an OPEB (other post-employment benefits) or a pension plan, you may not invest in anything other than investment grade bonds with seven years maturity or less.

Several school district boards in southeastern Wisconsin, even with this restriction, still managed to get into trouble in 2008. Whitefish Bay, along with four other school districts, suffered losses of nearly $200 million from investments in Collateralized Debt Obligation (CDO) securities. These securities, of course, were made up of mortgage-backed securities, which fell into default *en masse* as a result of the housing bubble. They had been sold to these organizations under the guise of "just like buying treasuries for seven years", but promised to earn a higher return. David Noack, a former senior vice president with Stiefel Nicholas, assured the members of the business staff and boards that "there would have to be a major economic crisis akin to '15–20 Enrons'" for the school districts to lose money.[5]

One thing the law did not restrict was the use of leverage, or the ability to borrow money for the purpose of investing to "amplify" the return. In this case, the school districts invested $35 million and then borrowed the rest—$165 million—to fund the entire investment. The problem with leverage is that it cuts both ways, magnifying both positive and negative returns, and the downside in this case was enormous. The case was eventually settled by the SEC, and the total cash recovered was close to $64 million, plus the debt was forgiven in the process. It was the second largest civil settlement in state history.[6]

---

[3] Pickering, Octavius (1831). *Harvard College and Massachusetts General v. Francis Amory. Reports of Cases Argued and Determined in the Supreme Judicial Court of Massachusetts, Vol. IX.* Boston: Hilliard, Gray, Little ad Wilkins. pp. 446–465.

[4] The Employee Retirement Income Security Act of 1974 (ERISA) is a federal law that sets minimum standards pension plans to protect the beneficiaries of those plans.

[5] SEC v. David W. Noack and Stiefel Nicholas & Co., Inc., filed 10/05/12 https://www.sec.gov/divisions/enforce/claims/docs/stifel-complaint.pdf

[6] Rumage, Jeff, "Whitefish Bay schools recoup failed $1.2M investment", Milwaukee Journal-Sentinel, December 15, 2016 https://www.jsonline.com/story/news/local/whitefish-bay/2016/12/15/whitefish-bay-schools-recoup-failed-12m-investment/95347966/

The Whitefish Bay School Board case points to another obstacle that boards face in fulfilling their fiduciary duty—**Asymmetry of knowledge**. Given the complexity of the many investment products available, boards must rely on the knowledge and advice of outside professionals. In this case, it's difficult not to question the knowledge—and ethics—of the advisor. No doubt the advisor understood his and his company's fees and commissions on the sale. Even if Noack had been a fiduciary, and he was not (he was a securities broker in this transaction), it might not have made a difference, because it is unlikely that he truly understood the risks either. It sounds ludicrous to say "20 Enrons". But many people believed that the triple A tranche of CDOs, at the time dubiously rated by Moody's and S&P, were safe like US treasuries. However, Chris as an investment professional and having provided advice and counsel to dozens of organizations over the years, and Sarah as a researcher and teacher on the effect of leverage, believe the heavy use of leverage crosses over into speculative—and imprudent—behavior.

So, as a governing fiduciary, how does one ensure one is acting in the position of a prudent investor, and not as an improvident speculator? This is a judgment call, but we think there are a couple of tests to be applied on this issue:

1. Does the investment offer a low probability of a high return? Or does the investment offer a more probable, albeit lower, reasonable rate of return?
2. Is it possible that the entire initial investment could be lost?
3. What percentage of the total portfolio is being placed at risk in this investment? How does the investment provide diversification among the other investment allocations? Does it raise or lower overall portfolio risk?
4. How much *total* leverage, if any, is being employed? Even if leverage is not an intentional component in a strategy, it could still be implicit or present especially in the use of derivatives.

This doesn't mean that governing boards should avoid risk. Quite the contrary, risk is an inherent part of investing, and can lead to higher returns over the long run. It's inevitable with 20–20 hindsight, that there will be poor investments made along the way. But it is the job of the governing fiduciary to make certain that the risks are understood as well as possible in advance and will not be catastrophic to the portfolio should they occur.

So, after the fiduciary has applied prudent judgment in the selection of investment professionals (staff or outside experts), or in the investments themselves, what else is important?

We answer this question by examining when fiduciaries and boards have run into legal problems. First, beneficiaries have legal rights. William Payne and Patrick Spangler in a 2012 legal brief describe in detail the litigation landscape for public pensions.[7] They begin with the observation that since the 1960s state courts have turned from the earlier view that pension benefits were "gratuities" that could be decreased or eliminated in retirement to the present view that, like private pensions, public pensions are "contract rights". They cite how several states, for example, Illinois and New Mexico, amended their constitutions to explicitly provide protection for public pensions as enforceable contract rights. They list the common types of litigation, all of which involve some form of benefit reduction or increase in contributions[8]:

- Cost of living adjustment changes
- Increased contribution rates
- Changes in calculation of benefits or eligibility
- Retiree health contributions and benefits

Second, as a fiduciary, trustees can get into trouble with investment decisions where they have a real or perceived conflict of interest. Kathleen Paisley, in a 1985 article that appeared in the *Yale Law and Policy Review,* called for the need for federal regulation of trustee investment decisions.[9] She identifies two main duties of the trustees: (1) to act at all times with strict loyalty to participants and their beneficiaries; and (2) to administer the funds of the trust prudently. She cites the case of *Withers v. Teachers Retirement System,* which involved a decision by the New York pension board to purchase $850 million of New York City municipal bonds. While in this case the court upheld the decision by the trustees, it was clear in examining the facts of the case the city would have gone bankrupt were it not for this purchase. Paisely was critical of the court's decision stating "the court examined the merits of the individual investment decision without considering its effect on the trust's overall portfolio of assets".[10]

---

[7] Payne, William T. and Spangler, Patrick W., "Public Employee Pension Litigation: Legal Landscape", 012 ABA Mid-Winter Meeting – Breakout Session, p.1.

[8] Ibid., p. 7.

[9] Paisley, Kathleen, "Public Pension Funds: The Need for Federal Regulation of Trustee Investment Decisions", Yale Law and Policy Review, Vol. 4, Issue 1, Article 10, 1985.

[10] Ibid., pp. 193–194.

In general, according to Robert A. Kutcher, common fiduciary breaches come in several forms[11]:

- Self-dealing (i.e., through conflict of interest or reaping of extra profits);
- Usurpation of business or corporate opportunity;
- Misappropriation of funds or property;
- Neglect, imprudence, or want of skill (e.g., failure to administer trust property as a prudent administrator, failure to properly diversify ERISA plan investments, or improper reliance on professionals);
- Failure to act in another's best interest;
- Misrepresentation/omission as to a statement of fact (e.g., financial condition/statement of affairs);
- Inducement;
- Breach of an assumed duty (e.g., to provide accurate information);
- Misuse of confidential information/breach of confidentiality;
- Misuse of superior knowledge;
- Failure to disclose;
- Aiding and abetting or acting in concert with another rendering inappropriate advice (e.g., bad business or investment advice); and
- Misuse of superior or influential position

In terms of understanding or evaluating the severity of a breach within the context of ERISA plans, Eric Chason explains the Supreme Court's view on this[12]:

> *An ERISA fiduciary who harms or abuses plan assets (e.g., by negligent investing) must make the plan whole by paying either damages or restitution. Trust beneficiaries may seek similar redress for breach of trust. Yet, unlike trust law, ERISA imposes fiduciary duties extending beyond the management and distribution of property. ERISA fiduciaries have discretion to pay or deny claims for benefits, and a wrongful denial of benefits can devastate an employee and her covered dependents. Fiduciary breaches that harm plan assets warrant full relief. Breaches that do not harm plan assets warrant only "appropriate equitable relief," which excludes most forms of monetary relief according to the Court.*

---

[11] Kutcher, Robert A., "Breach of Fiduciary Duties", *Business Torts Litigation, Second Edition*, American Bar Association, 2005, p. 11, David A. Soley, Robert Y. Gwin, and Ann E. Georgehead, editors.

[12] Chason, Eric D., "Redressing All ERISA Fiduciary Breaches Under Section 409 (a)", *William & Mary Law School Scholarship Repository*, College of William and Mary Law School, 2010, p. 148.

Table 3.1 Types of public pension legal cases

1	Investments: frauds
2	Investments: breaking agreements/duties
3	Benefit management/disbursement issues
4	Plan practical operations issues
5	Minor statutory duties regarding operations
6	Ulterior investment concerns
7	Unknown cases

Merker, Christopher Kinne, "Asset Owner Governance and Fiduciary Effectiveness: The Case of Public Pension Plans" (2017). *Dissertations (2009 -)*. 713, http://epublications.marquette.edu/dissertations_mu/713, p. 62

This general "doctrine of harm" from ERISA helps inform the evaluation of various types of cases based on their harms. In our legal research on pension plans, we examined close to 2500 cases. We constructed a severity variable that categorizes seven case types found in the data we collected on public pension plans, ranging from the most harmful, fraud, to the least harmful, minor statutory duties regarding operations. A final category of filed, but unknown cases was also included. The details of every case, often depending on the early stages of a case, are not always known. See Table 3.1.

Denial of benefits was the most frequent type of case. Cases involving security fraud was the next most frequent, indicating that boards need to be aware that when they lack proficiency on a particular investment being pitched to them, they should rely on the advice of conflict-free advisors. Not surprisingly, there was an increase in these types of cases after 2008. We also found that breach of fiduciary duty cases increased during this time. In sum, these findings reflect both the ethical and legal obligations inherent in fiduciary duty. Good corporate governance practices ensure that both are fulfilled.

4

Good Governance

Group effectiveness is a topic of ongoing interest in the management field. How effective organizations operate, ranging from small teams to large corporations, is a field of inquiry that is virtually endless in its theories and case examinations. Within this broad field of research, we have homed in on the boards responsible for the management of large pools of financial assets.

The record of effectiveness of these groups is mixed. One crucial measure of effectiveness is the rate of return performance of the assets under the board's stewardship. Looking only at public pensions from our initial study from 2008 to 2012, the range of annualized returns across the entire sample was −4.5–15%.

Even accounting for differences in asset allocation and investment objectives, these results show enormous disparity in performance, and on a dollar basis represent an opportunity cost in the billions. What is it about these groups, and the individuals that comprise them, that can drive such wide-ranging results?

The answer lies in how these groups organize (**governance structure**), the people that reside on the boards and committees of these organizations (**human factors**), and how they interact with each other and the consultants, other service providers, and the money managers with whom they work (**group processes**).

A 1995 study posed the question to US pension fund executives what they thought was the "excellence shortfall" in their organization; that is, if known barriers to excellence could be removed, how much might long-term

© The Author(s) 2019
C. K. Merker, S. W. Peck, *The Trustee Governance Guide*,
https://doi.org/10.1007/978-3-030-21088-5_4

performance improve?[1] The median response was 66 basis points (0.66%). For a long time, the working assumption in the area of governance is that better forms of it will translate into better performance. Yet there was no clear evidence of this. Tim Hatton, in his 2005 book on fiduciary practices, said that while there is no guaranteed improvement in performance from better process, it was, he suspected, a likely outcome.

In 2017, we updated our original study and were able to quantify from 17 governance factors that a one unit increase in the governance index score (fiduciary effectiveness quotient, or FEQ) saw a commensurate increase in annualized performance of 36 basis points (or 0.36%). This performance was in excess of the return that would have been earned given the plan's asset allocation. So, moving to the next quintile of governance performance, or roughly a ten-unit change, translated into an improvement of annualized performance of 3.60%. In economic and dollar terms, a 1% difference in return in our sample saw on average a $10.3 million reduction in annual required contributions by the state or local governments, a huge difference.

What were the drivers of this improvement?

Let's start with Clark and Urwin's 2008 observation that the members of boards are generally faced at best with an unevenness of knowledge of investments, are subject to biases, lack focus, and are overwhelmed by the sheer range of issues. Are there institutional or structural factors in the way that boards are organized that can buttress these issues? This is where our initial study focused to see if there were certain factors that drove improvements in outcomes.

A 2015 survey of pension organizations by Ambachtsheer and McLaughlin highlighted three areas that boards find most challenging[2]:

1. Board selection and improvement processes are flawed in many cases.
2. Board oversight needs to be more clearly defined and executed.
3. Competition for senior management and investment talent is often hampered by uncompetitive compensation structures.

Table 4.1 provides a summary of the highest and lowest ranked statements from that survey.

---

[1] Ambachtsheer, Boice, Ezra, McLaughlin (1995), "Excellence Shortfall in Pension Fund Management: Anatomy of a Problem", unpublished working paper.

[2] https://www.top1000funds.com/wp-content/uploads/2015/02/Pension-Governance-and-LT-Investing.pdf

Table 4.1 Five highest and lowest agreement statements from the 2015 KPA Advisory Survey

Survey highest agreement statements
My governing fiduciaries do a good job of representing the interests of plan stakeholders
Developing our investment policy required considerable effort on the part of the governing fiduciaries and me and it reflects our best thinking
There is a clear allocation of responsibilities and accountabilities for fund decisions between the governing fiduciaries and the pension investment team
My governing fiduciaries hold me accountable for our performance and do not accept sub-par performance
My governing fiduciaries approve the necessary resources for us to do our work

Survey lowest agreement statements
I have the authority to retain and terminate investment managers
Compensation levels in our organization are competitive
My governing fiduciaries have superior capabilities relevant knowledge, experience, intelligence, skills necessary to do their work
Our fund has an effective process for selecting, developing, and terminating its governing fiduciaries
Performance-based compensation is an important component of our organizational design

https://www.top1000funds.com/wp-content/uploads/2015/02/Pension-Governance-and-LT-Investing.pdf Ambachtsheer, Keith and McLaughlin, John, "How Effective is Pension Fund Governance Today? And Do Pension Funds Invest for the Long-term? Findings from a New Survey." KPA Advisory LTD, January, 2015

The main takeaways from that survey highlight issues around role clarity, policy orientation, professionalism, and process: All items that we will discuss below.

Components of Good Governance

Industry experts agree that good governance is an important determinant of long-term success. Willis Towers Watson stated that "organizations with effective retirement plan governance are better equipped to manage potential retirement plan risks, protect against fiduciary liabilities and capture opportunities to improve structures, strategies and metrics".

It sounds very compelling, but not particularly helpful. What does "effective plan governance" mean? How do we know it when we see it, and if we don't have it, how do we get it? How can the pursuit of good governance become a practical exercise within the reach of any organization, no matter how large or small?

Organizations must start by understanding what comprises good governance, then come up with a way of evaluating the organization's governance, and finally apply best practices for improvement through that process.

So, what is governance exactly? A longer definition would describe the establishment and implementation of policies by a board that oversees the overall organization for the purposes of enhancing the viability and prosperity of it for a certain group of people (e.g., beneficiaries, shareholders, etc.). In the context of managing pensions or other pools of assets (e.g., foundations and endowments), governance is simply codified and structured group investor behavior that drives ongoing organizational performance.

Ask any industry observer what matters on the topic of corporate governance, and you will get a different answer every time. As researchers, while we had an idea from the corporate governance literature regarding what matters, we didn't know exactly when it came to the governance of asset ownership organizations what matters most in this context. We started collecting data and created the first ever governance database of public pension plans. For two and half years, we collected data on 42 governance variables from dozens and dozens of public pension plans' meeting minutes. We continue to update that database.

In addition, we collected data on what actually pension plan boards did as recorded in the minutes, rather than relying on survey data, which can suffer from bias, both of the researcher and the respondent. The list of governance variables was then further narrowed down to 17 core variables. After an in-depth examination of these core variables, we ascertained seven key drivers, comprising a final index measure of governance, the Fiduciary Effectiveness Quotient™ or FEQ™.

Using this index, we found that governance matters. When constructing a model of governance of public pension plans like corporate governance, we ascertained robust statistical relationships amongst the governance variables and performance outcomes (i.e., investment returns, funding ratios, and other financial variables). With respect to investment returns, the pattern was clear, as shown in Fig. 4.1.

Here we see all public pensions in our sample sorted by the FEQ. They are then broken into quintiles, top quintile being the top 20% and bottom quintile, the bottom 20%. When we overlay the five-year investment returns, we found mean investment returns for plans that scored in the top quintile of the index outperformed the bottom quintile nearly 2 to 1 on average, with a difference of approximately 3.5% in investment return per year. In the world of pension investing, a performance gap that large is enormous and has all kinds of implications for future funding and viability.

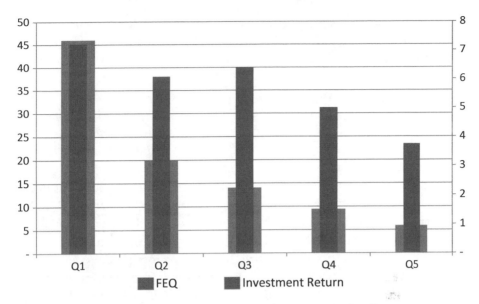

Fig. 4.1 Public pension fund performance by FEQ™ quintile, five-year average. (Merker, Christopher Kinne, "Asset Owner Governance and Fiduciary Effectiveness: The Case of Public Pension Plans" (2017). *Dissertations (2009 -)*. 713, http://epublications. marquette.edu/dissertations_mu/713, p. 195)

Why does it matter? Can't the sponsor or employees simply make up the difference with contributions? Shouldn't they simply be making up the difference? Some have argued that it is not the investment returns that are the problem, but that the state sponsors themselves have simply been underfunding for too long. The state of Massachusetts Employee Retirement System is 63% funded, well below the average, but its returns have been among the top quartile in recent years.[3] So is this a fiduciary issue or a budgetary one? Clearly it is not a fiduciary issue in this example, but across the country it could be either, or it could be both. On average, in recent years *two-thirds* of the annual required contribution has come from investment returns, 10% from employees and a quarter from employers.[4] Both adequate funding and effective fiduciaries need to be functioning for plans to be prepared for the demographic headwinds facing every plan across America and much of the developed world.

For fiduciaries to be effective, they need to pay attention to governance. Specifically, from our study, we identified seven main drivers of effective

---

[3] According to data from the Boston College Center for Retirement Research.
[4] Source: JP Morgan (2016) – average percentage contribution of the last five years.

governance. These drivers or factors are measured by a constellation of variables, and factors can share variables that provide different ways of measuring the factor. The seven drivers or factors are:

1. **Professionalism** – This driver is a measure of the level of professionalism within the organization. Examples of variables that comprise it: To what extent is the consultant involved in guiding and informing the process? How often does the board meet and for how long? To what extent is the board documenting and disclosing its activities and decisions? How much board representation is there on the investment and audit committees? What are the substantive matters being discussed at the board level?
2. **Board Composition** – How large is the board? A large board makes it easier to construct committees and get a diversity of opinions. But too large a board can allow members to shrink away from participation. What is the mix of the board? Whose interests are most represented: Those of the sponsor (e.g., company or municipal government), those of the beneficiaries (e.g., retiree or union representation) or someone with an independent viewpoint? What are the backgrounds of the trustees? Do they have the proper training and experience for what they are charged with overseeing?
3. **Engagement** – Another important driver is the degree of engagement by the board members, staff, and consultant. How long do meetings last? Is everyone participating and engaged in the process? How much turnover is happening at the leadership or chair level? At the consultant level? Strong leadership is critical to keeping the other board members engaged in the governance process. Also, do the individuals on the board have time for engagement, or are they busy people managing multiple demands and not able to devote enough time to the issues at hand? Is the board over-involved relying too little on the advice of staff and investment consultants?
4. **Staff** – Is there enough staff or employee representation? Having professional staff serving on the board, or at least attending the meetings, is important from the standpoint of having people closest to the operation there to inform the board of ongoing activity and remain connected to oversight and decision-making.
5. **Institutional Knowledge** – This driver represents the continuity within the organization itself. How much professional experience do board members have? To what extent is the board itself and the consultant turning over each year? High rates of turnover can erode knowledge and continuity. Too little turnover can indicate a lack of fresh ideas coming into the process. One would expect that funds, especially those with access to good benchmarking information, would tend to herd together and follow the

same or similar investing path. It turns out the opposite is true, and many invest very differently as compared to their peers over time.

Changeover and staff may be a reason for variance in allocation and churn in activity. A couple of years ago, CalPERS announced very publicly it was getting out of its hedged and illiquid alternative investments.[5] Today that fund is back where it started.[6] The main difference: a new chief investment officer. One problem, particularly in the public funds' arena, is that compensation is not on par with other jobs in finance, and so retention of key staff remains a perennial issue.

6. **Diligence** – This is defined by the extent of diligence and thoroughness of the organization in exercising its governance process and making decisions. Underlying measures include participation of the consultant, extent of meeting documentation, involvement and direction by staff, and key discussion points.

7. **Transparency** – This final driver represents the quality of the disclosures to stakeholders. The more transparent the system, the more likely the system will be held to a higher standard. This transparency can come in the form of financial and performance reports and filings, publicly available meeting minutes and policy documents, transcripts and publicly available videos, press releases, and meetings with stakeholders, just to name a few examples. We found in our research that transparency across organizations was relatively inconsistent. For example, our ability to collect data on all organizations was limited by the amount of disclosure being made. Of the 163 largest systems in the country, in our initial study we were able to collect data on just over a third.

Further, in our first year of conducting our governance survey, reported below, we had a relatively low response rate. We are hopeful over time this improves as organizations become more aware of governance as a key issue, but for now that remains another sign of a system that remains relatively opaque and inaccessible.

The lack of transparency is particularly striking when compared to corporate disclosures. The Securities and Exchange Commission (SEC) in regulating public companies requires regular and extensive disclosure of the biographical information of their board members. Despite the trillions of dollars invested by public pension plans, there is little or no disclosure about who is on the board and how decisions are made.

---

[5] Fitzpatrick, Dan, "Calpers to Exit Hedge Funds: Pension Plan to Shed $4 Billion Investment to Simplify Its Assets, Reduce Costs", *Wall Street Journal*, September 15, 2014.

[6] Jacobius, Arlene, "CalPERS allocates $2.5 billion to alternatives, fixed income", *Pensions & Investments*, February 6, 2018.

Table 4.2 Results of the 2018 US public pension governance survey

Topic	Finding
Self-assessment	A vast majority of organizations indicated they conduct governance self-assessment either infrequently or not at all
Use of investment policies	Nearly 80% of organizations are using some form of investment policy
Review of policies	Typically reviewed every year or two
Diversity	Women, while in the minority, are still better represented than minorities, which tend to be a low percentage of board composition
Compensation	Only about a quarter of organizations see some form of board compensation for service
Training	Most conduct some training, typically on an annual basis
Background in investments	While half believe they have a medium to high level of professional experience on the board, at least a third of all boards also say they have low representation of skill and experience on the board
Expense	A wide range of investment expense structures exist

Pay-to-play in the industry, the practice of making political contributions or paying kick-backs or other perks to obtain or retain business, is an issue that pops up again and again across the industry. Ensuring arm's-length relationships with third parties is part of being transparent and acting with the highest degree of integrity and independence.

As part of best practices, there are other aspects that also should be considered in addition to these drivers including use of investment policies, board diversity, compensation, managing conflicts of interests, among others. Results from our **2018 US Public Pension Governance Survey** are listed in Table 4.2, showing current practice across several areas of governance. Again, response rates were low, so these results should not be regarded as statistically significant, and therefore not necessarily representative of the overall population.

Putting Knowledge into Practice

Taking what we learned through our research, the next step was to apply it in a way that could be useful for the organization itself. To accomplish this, we had to do two things: (1) find a way to efficiently and accurately collect the information from organizations to help them evaluate their practices; and (2) assist them with comparing their results with their peers. There are many board assessment instruments in the market to help the board undertake a

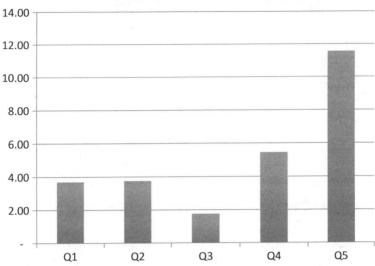

Five Year Average FEQ - Board Chair Turnover (in Percent)

Fig. 4.2 Board chair turnover. (Merker, Christopher Kinne, "Asset Owner Governance and Fiduciary Effectiveness: The Case of Public Pension Plans" (2017). *Dissertations (2009 -).* 713, http://epublications.marquette.edu/dissertations_mu/713, p. 230)

self-assessment. However, peer benchmarking is more difficult to find. We designed a system that accomplishes both goals.

One example of the assessment reporting shown in Fig. 4.2 is leadership turnover of the board, or the rate at which we see leadership changes within the organization. As noted, at higher levels this can impact overall continuity and engagement, and ultimately organizational performance. Lower levels of turnover are a feature of upper quintile organizations, with the highest level of turnover found in the bottom fourth and fifth quintiles.

In our study we also found that top FEQ™ organizations meet more often and for about three hours; have about 20% annual turnover of trustees, 25% turnover in an investment consultant when they use one; meeting minutes about 25 pages in length; nine board members; 83% attendance; and spend more time discussing investments.

Other Key Areas

With those as key drivers, what does an overall governance assessment need to consider? Table 4.3 summarizes important areas for every board to examine, according to Canadian governance expert, Mel Gill.

Table 4.3 Important governance topics for board assessment

Board structure: Policies and procedures, roles and responsibilities, membership and terms, committee structure, that is, executive, audit, investment, governance, and nominations, so on

Organizational culture: Rules and norms, culture of collaboration, promotion of dissent, trust and open communication

Responsibilities: Mission and planning, financial stewardship, human resources, performance monitoring and accountability, community representation and advocacy, and risk management

Board process: Board development (education) and management

Gill, Mel, *Governing for Results: A Directors Guide to Good Governance*, Trafford Publishing, 2005

Practitioner Focus: Board Self-Assessment

Studies have demonstrated that the mere act of board self-assessment has a positive impact on board performance. Review and documentation of board policy is important from the standpoint of creating a framework for board activity. However, the act of self-evaluation, itself, is an important element of board governance. Properly implemented, not only does it create the opportunity for boards to identify gaps in knowledge, but also to pinpoint differences of opinion between members, staff, and the senior executive or board chair.

Understanding what is driving those differences is key for the board leader or group facilitator. This can then allow issues to be raised to drive an awareness that can either facilitate an opportunity to address in open forum or through targeted board education. Either way the board is engaged and informed in a constructive manner.

There are a number of instruments in the market to perform board self-assessments. These include Board Source's board self-assessment tool, which is utilized especially in the nonprofit arena, or the Governance Self-Assessment Checklist (GSAC), which was originally developed by Mel Gill in conjunction with the University of Ottawa in the early 2000s, and is now available through our company, Fund Governance Analytics, in a brand-new digital format.

Once a board goes through a baseline evaluation, which takes typically no longer than 30 minutes using a governance assessment instrument, a board can then engage in a deeper self-assessment with board members and senior staff that reviews additional topics, which, using other board self-assessment tools, can include: further analysis of board structure, board and organizational culture, board responsibilities, and board process.

Making board governance a standing item for annual review helps the organization identify areas for training and development, track improvements over time and allows the setting of new goals for the coming year.

As Mark Goyder, founder of Tomorrow's Company, once noted so eloquently about the importance of governance and leadership to any organization:

> Governance and leadership are the yin and the yang…without governance you risk tyranny, fraud and personal fiefdoms. If you have governance without leadership you risk atrophy, bureaucracy and indifference.

Part II

The Second Imperative:
*Be Knowledgeable and Beware
of Common Errors*

5

Human Error and Behavioral Finance

What is human error? Human error means that something has been done that was "not intended by the actor; not desired by a set of rules or an external observer; or that led the task or system outside its acceptable limits".[1] In short, it is a deviation from intention, expectation, or desirability. Logically, human actions can fail to achieve their goal in two different ways: the actions can go as planned, but the plan can be inadequate, leading to mistakes; or, the plan can be satisfactory, but the performance can be deficient, leading to slips and lapses. However, a mere failure is not an error if there had been no plan to accomplish anything in particular.

We can further identify five common types of human error[2]:

- Errors of commission—these are the most obvious, where the operator takes the wrong action.
- Errors of omission—this is where the operator neglects to take the right action.
- Extraneous acts—the operator takes an action, when doing nothing would have been the preferred course.
- Sequential errors—the operator takes perhaps the right action, in the wrong order.
- Timing errors—the operator takes the right action, but at the wrong time.

---

[1] Senders, J.W. and Moray, N.P. (1991) Human Error: Cause, Prediction, and Reduction Lawrence Erlbaum Associates, p. 25.

[2] Guastello, Stephen, Human Factors Engineering and Ergonomics: A Systems Approach, Boca Raton, FL, CRC Press.

© The Author(s) 2019
C. K. Merker, S. W. Peck, *The Trustee Governance Guide*,
https://doi.org/10.1007/978-3-030-21088-5_5

Chris would add one to the list, particularly in competitive situations, the so-called unforced error, as typically described in tennis.[3] This is where a loss on the court results only from one's own blunder and not from the skill or action of the other player. This is relevant especially when considered in the context of the zero-sum game of securities trading, where every dollar "won" by one trader must be lost by another.[4]

In investment management, where risk management is a central concept, human error in practice is most narrowly defined as "operational risk". According to KPMG, operational risk in banks, funds, and insurance companies is[5]:

[d]efined as the risk of loss resulting from inadequate or failed internal processes, people and systems or from external events. This definition includes legal risk, but excludes strategic and reputational risk.

As an example, in 2001 the State of Wisconsin Investment Board (SWIB) made a clerical error in a performance calculation that cost the pension approximately $4.5 million when determining a payout to the Milwaukee Public School system's supplemental early retirement plan. In this case, a simple decimal error was the culprit. The board told the pension plan administrator that the February 2001 all-stock variable return was −0.089%, when actually it was −8.90%, and the return for the fixed fund, which contained a stock and bond mix, was −0.046%, when actually it was −4.60%.[6]

According to the state board's former chief operating officer, Ken Johnson, "It wasn't the technology that wasn't performing correctly, it was a case of human error. The decimal point was put in the wrong spot when the person read the return off the report – the number e-mailed [was wrong]".

While operational risk is a simple concept to understand, the behavioral finance literature has focused on another form of risk (behavioral risk) to explain irrationality in financial decision-making.

Behavioral finance is a relatively new field that seeks to combine behavioral and cognitive psychological theory with conventional economics and finance to provide explanations for why people make irrational financial decisions.[7]

---

[3] Krames, Jeffrey A., *The Unforced Error: Why Some Managers Get Promoted While Others Get Eliminated*, Portfolio, 2009

[4] http://247wallst.com/investing/2007/03/08/why_trading_is_/

[5] https://www.kpmg.com/lu/en/services/advisory/risk-consulting/financialregulatoryreporting/documents/operational-risk.pdf

[6] http://www.globalaging.org/pension/us/socialsec/milwaukeeplan.htm

[7] http://www.investopedia.com/university/behavioral_finance/

Table 5.1 Two forms of human error in investment management

	Form	Safeguard
Operational risk	Discrete	Procedural/system enhancement
Behavioral risk	Continuous	Governance structure/process enhancement

Merker, Christopher Kinne, "Asset Owner Governance and Fiduciary Effectiveness: The Case of Public Pension Plans" (2017). *Dissertations (2009 -).* 713, http://epublications.marquette.edu/dissertations_mu/713, p. 86

These two forms of error present in investment management, operational risk and behavioral risk or error in human decision-making, are very different forms of error. Operational risk can be more easily controlled and safeguarded against through audits, procedures, and practices; behavioral risk is more subjective, ambiguous, and difficult to judge in practice, and requires structural and process adjustments to limit it. It is often only known after the fact when reviewing performance against peers or market benchmarks. See Table 5.1 for a summary.

Finally, there is, of course, a range of tolerance for human error in human affairs. This largely depends whether there is a "second chance" attribute, an opportunity to recover from the error. The examples of zero tolerance in human error are countless, mostly where human life is at stake: surgery, nuclear power, air travel, heavy construction, and so on. Of course, the financial and reputational costs are also of major importance.

Todd and Walsh describe common oversight mistakes of pension committees.[8] As discussed earlier, oversight of plan investments is a fundamental duty of boards.

Focusing on Investment Manager Selection Over the Asset Allocation Decision They reference investment research such as the 1986 Brinson, Hood, and Beebower study, which asserts that investment outcomes are as much as 90% determined by the asset allocation decision, making this the primary lever by which investors can impact long-term performance.[9] Their admonition is that many committees get bogged down in a "this versus that" manager discussion, and lose sight of the bigger picture. We will delve a lot more into this topic in Chap. 12.

---

[8] Todd, Richard and Walsh, Martin, "Avoid Common Pension Oversight Mistakes", Society for Human Resource Management, August 5, 2013.

[9] Brinson, Gary P., Hood, Randolph L., Beebower, Gilbert L., "Determinants of Portfolio Performance", *Financial Analysts Journal* (July–August 1986): 39–44.

Not Focusing on Plan Liabilities Plan sponsors can fall into the trap of not forming investment policy that considers long-term liabilities. The interplay of liabilities and time horizon are important considerations when making the asset allocation decision. An allocation that does not tolerate short-term volatility in asset classes such as equity and alternatives may undermine the ability of the investment pool to meet liability payments in the future without significant additional contributions by the sponsor to make up the shortfall.

Backward-Looking Bias There are many biases that individuals and groups are subject to in investing. However, Todd and Walsh highlight this one given its all too common appearance with investment committees. It is a tendency to look in the rear-view mirror when making decisions, which causes them to increase their investments in asset classes that have performed well recently and avoid areas that have underperformed— also known in the business as "chasing the hot dot".

Lack of an Investment Policy Organizations that fail to produce and adhere to this governing document do so at their own peril. First, it protects fiduciaries from allegations by beneficiaries that they did not comply with their "duty of care" by demonstrating a piece of important evidence of a clear process. Secondly, it guides investment decision-making and action. A disciplined investment process is another key factor in driving effective results over time.

Dysfunctional Investment Committees Group dynamics are important in limiting and avoiding mistakes. A "bully" member may exert inordinate influence on a committee's investment decisions. A strong and fair committee chair is key to dampening this effect to build consensus toward effective decisions. Diversity of committees is important for avoiding groupthink. Relevant—and depth of—experience of the members of the committee must be adequate for successful evaluation of investment decisions.

Failure to Exercise the Duty of Loyalty Committee members must have a duty of loyalty to the plan and its beneficiaries only. Temptation to direct economic benefits of the plan to the employer or to third parties is a common conflict of interest to which members of committees and boards are subject. This was a topic we covered in Chap. 3.

Working with a Conflicted Advisor Likewise, organizations are often subject to working with a consultant or advisor who is conflicted by fee arrangements or internal corporate pressures. Such advisors may not be acting in the best interest of the plan, which can result in suboptimal outcomes. Not picking up on these conflicts is where committees regularly err.

However, one reason they are common is because many firms find themselves in the position, from the standpoint of economic incentive, of acting as both "manufacturer and distributor" of their own product, which structurally creates the conflict in the first place. The growth in registered investment advisors (RIAs), or independently run investment advisory businesses, has been a form of reaction to that conflict and has been a significant trend in the industry over the last several years.[10]

Behavioral Finance

Behavioral finance has changed the way we fundamentally view the investor. It has effectively challenged the rational expectations model of neoclassical economics. The theory asserts that people are not walking calculators, seeking optimality at every given point, but rather they are emotional decision-makers that are often lazy, rushed, or pressured, and therefore seemed doomed to repeat the same errors over and over.

Behavioral finance holds that investors tend to fall into predictable patterns of destructive behavior. In other words, they make the same mistakes repeatedly. Specifically, many investors damage their portfolios by under-diversifying; trading frequently; following the herd; favoring the familiar (domestic stocks, company (employer) stock, and glamour stocks); selling winning positions and holding on to losing positions (disposition effect); and succumbing to optimism, short-term thinking, and overconfidence (self-attribution bias).

One piece of substantial empirical evidence taken in aggregate is the plight of markets to repeat the creation—and eventual collapse—of market bubbles, also known as financial manias, which are characterized by first gradual and then sudden rapid expansion of prices in a commodity or asset class segment. This is not a new phenomenon, with two significant bubbles in the US over the last 15 years alone (e.g., 1999–2000 "dot com" bubble and the 2005–2007 housing bubble). The combined irrationality of investors is the driving factor in every asset bubble.

What lies behind investor irrationality? The nuts and bolts of investor behavior are the heuristics and biases that impel that behavior. In psychology, heuristics are simple, efficient rules, which people often use to form judgments and make decisions. They are mental shortcuts that usually involve focusing on one aspect of a complex problem and ignoring others. These rules

---

[10] http://wealthmanagement.com/rias/no-slowing-ria-growth

work well under most circumstances, but they can lead to systematic deviations from logic, probability, or rational choice theory.

The resulting errors are called "cognitive biases" and many different types have been documented (see below). These have been shown to affect people's choices in situations like valuing a house, deciding the outcome of a legal case, or making an investment decision. Heuristics usually govern automatic, intuitive judgments, but can also be used as deliberate mental strategies when working from limited information.

Combatting these biases, particularly in the governance setting, requires education and training. It also requires strong and engaged leadership to help foster an open and thoughtful arena for deliberation, debate, and communication. This may be a tall order for many groups that may only meet four times a year for a couple of hours at each meeting.

The identified and documented behavioral finance biases are as follows:

Active trading. Barber and Odean show how active traders can underperform the market. Active trading correlates with overconfidence.[11] Some gender differences may be a driver of ineffective behavior. They find a correlation between male overconfidence and excessive trading, particularly when comparing single men and single women. Because women are less likely to indulge in excessive trading, they often outperform men.

Belief persistence. This is the tendency among people to hold on to beliefs long after the basis for those beliefs has been substantially discredited.

Causal attribution theory. Another tendency among people to attribute above average credit for group success or below average responsibility for group failure.

Confirmation bias. A bias related to belief persistence, where the decision-maker seeks out information to confirm the original theory or belief system.

Conformity bias. In every aspect of their lives, people take cues from those around them about the proper way to act. This bias strongly pushes people to conform their judgments to the judgments of their reference group. This produces a poor group decision-making process, what Shiller described as "conservative compliance with broadly perceived conventional wisdom and past procedures".[12]

---

[11] Barber, Brad M. and Odean, Terrance, "All that Glitters: The Effect of Attention and News on the Buying Behavior of Individual and Institutional Investors," *Review of Financial Studies* 21, no. 2 (April 2008): 785–818.

[12] Shiller, Robert, "Bubbles, Human Judgment and Expert Opinion", Cowles Foundation Discussion Paper No. 1303, May 2001.

Disposition effect. The tendency of investors is to sell winning positions and to hold onto losing positions to recoup losses on the losing positions.[13] *Myopic loss aversion* is a related concept, where investors evaluate their portfolios too frequently and make moves to avoid losses during periods of short-term volatility.[14]

Familiarity bias. People prefer to invest in what is familiar, favoring their own country, region, state, and company. This is also known as "equity home bias", which can lead to ignoring or eliminating a broad swath of potential investments across the investing universe and overconcentration in a specific geography.[15]

Framing. Psychologists have demonstrated how a simple reframing of a question can produce a completely different answer from the same respondent. For example, reframing an option in terms of a gain instead of loss can change a person's risk preference dramatically.

Groupthink. Conformity bias rears its ugly head in the form of groupthink. Pressures from superiors and peers can be reinforced by the tendency of members of a group to avoid introducing stress into unanimity by suppressing dissent and silencing critics. This leads to decisions that are not subject to an independent, deliberative, and thoughtful process.

Hindsight bias. This is the tendency, referred to earlier, of investors to look only at the most recent past returns in extrapolating future performance.[16]

Lack of knowledge and trust. Financial illiteracy and lack of trust in the financial markets may also play a role in people's unwillingness to engage in productive investing. Guiso et al. attribute limited participation in the stock market, particularly among wealthy investors, to a lack of trust and to the fear of being cheated by participants in the capital markets.[17] Subjective and cultural factors also determine how trusting people are, as well as whether and how much they are willing to invest.

Naive diversification. Investors are often subject to equally weighting every investment option available to them as they do not have the tools or under-

---

[13] Odean, Terrance, "Are Investors Reluctant To Realize Their Losses?" *Journal of Finance* 53, no. 5 (October 1998): 1775–98.

[14] Benartzi, Schlomo and Thaler, Richard (2007), "Heuristics and Biases in Retirement Savings Behavior", *Journal of Economic Perspectives*—Volume 21, Number 3—Summer 2007—Pages 81–104

[15] Huberman, Gur, "Familiarity Breeds Investment," *Review of Financial Studies* 14, no. 3 (Autumn 2001): 659–80.

[16] Kahneman, Daniel and Tversky, Amos; "Prospect Theory: An Analysis of Decision under Risk", *Econometrica*, 47(2), pp. 263–291, March 1979

[17] Guiso, Luigi, Sapienza, Paola, and Zingales, Luigi, "Trusting the Stock Market," *Journal of Finance* 63, no. 6 (December 2008): 2557–2600.

standing to understand differences in each investment. This is a common occurrence in 401(k) investing.[18]

Noise trading. This describes the activities of "an investor who makes decisions regarding buy and sell trades without the use of fundamental data". These investors generally have poor timing, follow trends, and overreact to good and bad news.[19]

Overconfidence. Errors caused by overoptimism may be exacerbated by overconfidence, an over-endowed sense of belief in one's self, capabilities, and decisions. Students, psychologists, engineers, stock analysts, financial analysts, investment bankers, and investors among many other categories of people have been shown to tend toward irrational confidence in the accuracy of their decisions.

Overoptimism. People have a tendency toward optimism, an expectation of positive outcomes. It can be so strong it can lead to misguided beliefs and imprudent decisions. In certain circumstances, it can also induce unethical conduct.

Self-serving bias. This is a decision-maker's bias to gather, process, and even recall information to advance perceived self-interest and to support pre-existing views.

Reluctance to save and invest. Mitchell and Utkus refer to an individual's preference for deferring or not deferring consumption based on an individual's subjective discount rate.[20] They define those who defer more and discount less as "exponential discounters" and those who save little or nothing and discount more as "hyperbolic discounters". Exponential discounters tend to assign a higher value to future money. This also relates to the concept of *bounded rationality*, or the flawed decisions people make because of limited time, information, and cognitive ability.

Sunk costs. Economists and accountants can demonstrate how consideration of sunk costs is an illogical exercise. Yet, people go to plays they do not want to, just because they already purchased the tickets. Worse yet, is that sunk costs can lead to an *escalation of commitment*, where more good money is poured in after bad. This can explain a lot of ineffective—and even cata-

---

[18] Shlomo Benartzi and Richard H. Thaler, "Naive Diversification Strategies in Defined Contribution Saving Plans," American Economic Review 91, no. 1 (March 2001): 79–98.

[19] Barber, Brad M. and Odean, Terrance, "All that Glitters: The Effect of Attention and News on the Buying Behavior of Individual and Institutional Investors," *Review of Financial Studies* 21, no. 2 (April 2008): 785–818.

[20] Mitchell, Olivia S. and Utkus, Stephen P., "Lessons from Behavioral Finance for Retirement Plan Design," *in Pension Design and Structure: New Lessons from Behavioral Finance*, ed. Mitchell and Utkus, 3–41 (Oxford, UK: Oxford University Press, 2004).

strophic—behavior, for instance rogue traders, and companies "doubling-down" on products that are failing in the marketplace.

Time-delay traps. People tend to emphasize the consequences of the near term over the long term. This tends toward short-termism in decision-making and a common inability to delay gratification. Successful investing most often requires a long-term approach.

Under-diversification. Related to familiarity bias, Statman explored the lack of diversification in US investors' equity portfolios.[21] Although mean-variance portfolio theory recommends that portfolios hold at least 300 stocks, the average investor holds only three or four, representing an extremely under-diversified portfolio. The typical investor's concentration in employer, large capitalization, and domestic stocks also works against the advantages of diversification.

We list these behavioral biases in Table 5.2. Consider using this as a check list when you are making investment decisions.

According to Robert Shiller, proof of the human capacity to make poor investment decisions on a massive scale, even among those we would deem experts, can be found particularly in the recurring pattern of investment bubbles and manias:

> *Those who manage university endowments have at their disposal some of the finest scholars, and university trustees who are drawn from the highest ranks of the business world. Who would presume to call these people foolish? But, that is what one would apparently have to do if one wishes to attribute the market behavior to human error.*[22]

Table 5.2 Summary of behavioral finance biases

Active trading	Lack of knowledge and trust
Belief persistence	Naive diversification
Causal attribution theory	Noise trading
Confirmation bias	Overconfidence
Conformity bias	Overoptimism
Disposition effect	Self-serving bias
Familiarity bias	Reluctance to save and invest
Framing	Sunk costs
Groupthink	Time-delay traps
Hindsight bias	Under-diversification

---

[21] Statman, Meir, "The Diversification Puzzle," *Financial Analysts Journal* 60, no. 4 (July–August 2004): 44–53.

[22] Shiller, Robert J. "Bubbles, Human Judgment, and Expert Opinion." *Financial Analysts Journal*, vol. 58, no. 3, 2002, pp. 18–26. *JSTOR*, www.jstor.org/stable/4480389

Practitioner Focus: How Much Endowment Is Enough?[23]

On the surface of it, the question seems silly. How can a school have too much endowment? After all, Harvard's endowment is approximately $36 billion and campaigns for additional gifts to its endowment continue to prosper. Driven by market performance and increasing personal wealth, college and independent school endowments continue to record strong growth. At the same time, tuition in these institutions continues to rise, suggesting that trustees are not looking to endowments as a means to curtail the growth in fees necessary to meet increasing operating costs. A notable exception is Williams College which, after watching its endowment triple since 1990, from $333 million to over $1 billion, decided not to raise tuition, room, board, and other fees for the 2000–2001 academic year. This unusual response perhaps reflects the growing criticism of colleges that raise tuition and fees in the face of burgeoning investment portfolios.

The question, how much endowment is enough, asks whether there is an optimum level of support that a school's endowment should provide to the operating budget and, if so, what level of endowment assets will provide that optimum level of support? If there is an optimum level of support, then a school should be able to identify it and, in concert with other policies, determine the portfolio value that will provide it. If there is not an optimum level of support and every dollar of endowment raised inures to the fiscal health of the institution, then it is clear that schools and colleges will seek to grow their endowments without limit.

Chris believes that the question is answerable and that it acquires strategic importance in light of the inherent competition that exists within a school's fund-raising priorities for operating versus capital gifts and, in the case of capital gifts, for gifts to physical capital and for gifts to financial capital. Each of these types of gift has a unique form and, usually, a characteristic size range. Annual fund gifts for operations are typically smaller and support operating needs. Gifts for physical capital generally fund new construction or extensive renovation and upgrades and are typically larger than gifts to operations. The principal of gifts to the endowment is always restricted in perpetuity with the investment return earned on those gifts either unrestricted or, typically, restricted to operating items (financial aid, faculty development, chairs of dis-

---

[23] Reprinted with permission from the author, Sorrel Paskin, National Association of Independent Schools (NAIS), https://www.nais.org/articles/pages/how-much-endowment-is-enough-3f-145452.aspx

tinguished teaching, etc.). Such gifts tend to be large and are of interest to a more limited pool of donors.

Clearly, as evidenced by practice, most schools seek all three kinds of gifts. Interestingly, schools set goals for the annual fund and for capital gifts to plant, but only rarely state a goal for endowment unless gifts to endowment are included within a capital campaign. The level of support provided by the annual fund is usually prescribed by the budget and takes into account past results. New construction and extensive renovation have identifiable costs. The figure included for the endowment component is not constructed so definitively, however. It is sometimes founded upon what the school feels the campaign can achieve in total and the perceived interests and capacities of those benefactors likely to give to endowment. The inclusion of endowment also establishes a kind of balance among the beneficiaries of the sought resources. Even in this case, however, one senses that this particular burst of enthusiasm for endowment, even if satisfied, will not result in the creation of an investment portfolio sufficient to meet the school's judgment of its need for financial capital. That amount of endowment perpetually remains out of reach.

In most independent day schools, parents are the principal source of philanthropy. Not only are they asked to pay substantial tuition and fees, but they are also called upon to make gifts to the annual fund, to fuel additions to plant, and to secure the future well-being of the institution through the perpetual support provided by gifts to endowment. Alumnus giving in day schools through grade 12 also supports these campaigns, but becomes a more significant player in boarding schools.

In recent years, capital costs associated with technology infrastructure and equipment have required substantial investment in plant. Additional plant investments have arisen from the need to retire deferred maintenance backlogs, to adapt existing space to new uses, and to add facilities desired by today's students and parents. At the same time, operating budgets have continued to rise, on average, about 1.5–2% above external CPI inflation, necessitating tuition increases averaging 5% per year and increases in the annual fund at about the same level. If parents are the principal source of gifts made to the school, then of necessity, the school must prioritize its fund-raising goals to ensure the success of each of the components of its annual campaigns. It is in this context of defining fund-raising goals and gift solicitation and allocation strategies that it makes sense to inquire into whether there is an optimum level of support a school should seek from its endowment.

The Role of Endowment in Maintaining Financial Equilibrium

At any point in time, the investment return on the school's endowment funds, whether unrestricted or restricted to specific operating functions, covers a certain percentage of the operating budget. Thus, a school with a $20 million operating budget and a $30 million endowment utilizing a 4.5% payout rate includes $1,350,000 of endowment investment return in the revenue stream of its operating budget. That level of endowment investment return represents 6.75% of the budget.

Maintaining long-run financial equilibrium with respect to endowment investment return means that absent new gifts, over time and on average, (in this example) 6.75% of the operating budget should continue to be supported by endowment investment return. Alternatively stated, in long-run financial equilibrium, the growth rates of investment principal, investment return, and the school's operating budget are all equal. The equilibrium payout (or spending) rate that produces that result is the equilibrium spending rate[24].

Equilibrium spending rate = real total return − real cost rise

(Note that the relation can also be expressed in nominal values. Since external inflation (CPI) increases the real total return and the real cost-rise to the same extent, the CPI value simply subtracts out.)

In the example above, if real total return is 6.0% (nominal total return = 9% if CPI = 3%) and if real cost-rise is 1.5% (nominal institutional inflation = 4.5% if CPI = 3%), then the equilibrium spending rate is 4.5%. This is the payout rate from the endowment investment return that is sustainable in the long run and that maintains the endowment's share of the operating budget, a condition of financial equilibrium. Thus, for an endowment to support an activity or a function in perpetuity, the growth of the endowment fund must be matched to the school's cost-rise average (the annual growth rate of the operating budget). This is the meaning of support in perpetuity—an endowment that grows at the rate of budget growth maintains its purchasing power over time; in this manner, the real value of the endowment is preserved.

---

[24] This formula assumes that the spending appropriation remains in the endowment portfolio and earns a return for the full year. In that case, the ending value of the endowment is given by the following expression: ending endowment = (1 + total return − spending rate) × (beginning endowment).

However, there is another reason to match the growth of the endowment fund to the school's cost-rise average. When the purchasing power of endowment funds is preserved, equity among past, present, and future generations of students is also preserved. In the words of Yale economist James Tobin, "The trustees of an endowed institution are the guardians of the future against the claims of the present. Their task is to preserve equity among generations. The trustees of an endowed [school] assume the institution to be immortal. They want to know, therefore, the rate of consumption from endowment that can be sustained indefinitely…. In formal terms, the trustees are supposed to have a zero rate of time preference."

Consuming endowment income so defined means in principle that the existing endowment can continue to support the same set of activities that it is now supporting. This rule says that current consumption should not benefit from the prospects of future gifts to endowment. Sustainable consumption rises to encompass an enlarged scope of activities when, but not before, capital gifts enlarge the endowment.[25]

Note that an overly conservative posture on the part of trustees, expressed in policies that require reinvestment of all endowment investment return or provide for spending rates that are less than the equilibrium spending rate, benefits future generations of students at the expense of the present generation. Given a balanced budget, less than the optimal allocation of endowment investment return to operating expense must result in an excessive tuition price if service levels are maintained or a reduction in service levels if growth in the tuition price is constrained.

Payout Policies

Payout or endowment return spending policies take a variety of forms throughout independent schools and colleges. Some schools spend investment yield (interest and dividends) only, reinvesting realized and unrealized gains; others spend a percentage of the ending market value of the endowment investment portfolio. In an effort to smooth the volatility associated with either of these approaches, many schools employ a moving average technique, spending a predetermined percentage of a three-year or five-year trailing average market value of the investment portfolio. Another approach

---

[25] Tobin, James. "What is Permanent Endowment Income?" *American Economic Review* 64. 1974. Quoted in Massey, William F. et al., *Resource Allocation in Higher Education*. Ann Arbor, University of Michigan Press, 1996. Pp. 93–94.

adopted by a smaller number of schools is to increase the amount spent each year by a preset increment (percentage factor) applied to last year's appropriation. Thus, if in academic year 2000–2001, the endowment investment return included in operations is $1,000,000 and the preset increment is 5%, then the appropriation for 2001–2002 would be $1,050,000. The amount of reinvestment delivered by a spend-only-yield policy bears no relation to the amount necessary to offset internal cost-rise; the actual amount reinvested may be more than or less than the amount required. Such a policy may also bind investment strategy to the school's need for current funds thereby dictating portfolio management strategy.

The ending market value technique is based upon total return and has the advantage of separating portfolio management issues from current spending needs. However, the results of its application are also subject to volatility. Consider that a portfolio invested 70% in equities and 30% in fixed income securities has an expected nominal total return of 9% (expected real return is 5.5%); however, expected volatility for this investment sector allocation is 12 percentage points (i.e., there is a one-in-three chance that annual investment return will fall outside the range of 5.5% +/− 12%). Such volatility can produce unacceptable swings both in the annual amount spent for operations and in the amount reinvested in the portfolio.

The moving average technique dampens volatility but increases the divergence between actual and equilibrium spending levels as the number of years included in the average increases. Moreover, the effect of a large total-return deviation in one year remains in the moving average with undiminished weight until it is dropped at the end of the last year included, thereby producing a kind of "jerkiness" in the determination of the actual spending level for that next year. Finally, while the preset increment method matches endowment return spending to the growth in the budget, it contains no "feedback" mechanism for deviations of total return from expectation and can result in spending levels in excess of the equilibrium rate and reinvestment levels below the amount necessary to maintain financial equilibrium. For example, if real portfolio return in a given year is −6.5% and the preset increment is 5% (i.e., the amount to be spent next year is 5% more than the amount spent this year), the amount spent as a percentage of ending portfolio value will significantly exceed the equilibrium spending rate.

It is possible to combine the moving-average and percentage-increment methods into a technique that exploits the strengths of each and minimizes their individual weaknesses. This hybrid method[26] is applied on a per-share

---

[26] Massey, William F. et al., *Resource Allocation in Higher Education*. Ann Arbor, University of Michigan Press, 1996. Pp. 107–108.

basis, not to the overall market value of the portfolio. The procedure simultaneously takes account of the equilibrium spending rate and the desired spending increment based upon budgetary growth. The actual spending appropriation resulting from the calculation tends to converge to its equilibrium value.

The calculation formula is actually an exponentially weighted moving average; the influence of each prior year's total return declines exponentially. For example, the weight applied to the current year's market value is 0.33, that for last year's is 0.332, the one for the previous year's is 0.333, and so on. This avoids the problem with the simple moving average technique that a given data point may vanish abruptly. Spending growth is continuously adjusted in response to market results. The method is applied through the following procedure:

1. Calculate per-share spending under the preset increment method, setting the escalator equal to the expected budget growth.
2. Calculate equilibrium rate spending, which is the product of the equilibrium spending rate and the beginning per-share market value.
3. Set next year's per-share spending equal to a weighted average of the preset increment and the equilibrium values. The weight applied to the equilibrium spending level usually runs between 0.25 and 0.4. A weight of 0.33 is used at Stanford and Yale. (See Hybrid Method, p. 48).

Managing the Endowment-Support Ratio

There is not a single, universal answer to the question, how much endowment is enough. Instead, each institution must make its own determination. It is clear, however, that a number of factors enter into that determination and that the strategic construction of those factors enables a school to rationally identify its optimum level of endowment support. Important to the decision framework is the endowment-support ratio, calculated as follows:

$$\text{Endowment support ratio} = \frac{\left[(\text{spending rate}) \times \left(\begin{array}{c}\text{beginning endowment}\\\text{market value}\end{array}\right)\right]}{[\text{operating budget for the year}]}$$

The endowment-support ratio is the strategic variable in determining the optimum level of endowment support. It reflects the fraction of the budget that is supported by endowment investment return. The answer to the question of the optimum level of support to be provided by the endowment is the determination of the optimum value for the endowment-support ratio. Managing the value of the endowment-support ratio should be a conscious process; its value should not be allowed to evolve as an unintended consequence of other policies. Basically, there are three levers available to establish and maintain this value. Each of these levers marks a further point of strategic decision-making: (1) the real budget growth rate; (2) the spending/reinvestment policy and total return earned on the portfolio; and (3) gifts and other additions to endowment.

The greater the budget growth rate the more upward pressure there is on the endowment-support ratio. Using the equilibrium-spending rate is a sufficient condition for maintaining the endowment-support ratio only when the budget is not growing faster than institutional cost-rise. The budget growth rate will normally exceed institutional cost-rise when present service levels are expanded beyond ordinary inflation (increasing faculty and staff numbers or enhancing benefits programs, for example) or when new programs or services are introduced. Absent service expansion, the equilibrium-spending rate should maintain the endowment-support ratio over time.

The amount of income and net gains reinvested affects the numerator of the endowment-support ratio by changing the beginning endowment market value. Therefore, reinvested income can offset the effect of real budget growth and stabilize the endowment-support ratio even in the face of increased services and programs. Adjustments to the portfolio asset mix that do not lead to inappropriate assumptions of risk can achieve this outcome. Reducing the spending rate also increases reinvestment, but at the expense of the initial endowment-support ratio.

A capital campaign is the most visible method of increasing the flow of gifts to endowment. As noted above, however, schools often add large unrestricted gifts and bequests to the endowment portfolio and operating surpluses may also be designated for long-term investment as endowment. In each of these situations, the trustees must make a choice between sometimes competing goals. In the case of a campaign, the decision may rest upon the allocation of goals between physical capital and financial capital. In the case of unrestricted gifts and operating surpluses, the decision is between current consumption and accumulating operating reserves or investing for the future. If the path of investment for the future is chosen, then a further decision must be made between which form of capital, physical or financial, will benefit from that investment.

If a school is growing in size and its budget is increasing to reflect that growth, maintaining the endowment-support ratio requires that new gifts be added to the endowment or that additional total return be reinvested in the portfolio. This implies that in the case of a growing school, any capital campaign (or private solicitation) should contain an endowment component. Again, if the board determines that the range or quality of services offered to students should be increased without a corresponding increase in enrollment or in price, an effective way to manage the added cost is to increase the endowment-support ratio over a specified period of years through an appropriate adjustment of fund-raising and resource allocation priorities.

Optimizing the Endowment-Support Ratio

A school has enough endowment when the accumulation and spending policies established by the trustees for the endowment portfolio maintain the value of the endowment-support ratio over time. The value of the ratio that is optimum for a given school is established by its long-range strategic plan. In constructing that plan, the trustees take into account the critical factors associated with the school's performance: enrollment change, planned initiatives including new programs and services, facilities needs and responses, market constraints and opportunities, institutional strengths and weaknesses. The strategic plan also models alternative futures based upon the different scenarios constructed.

The financial component of each future modeled includes estimates of revenue inflows derived from tuition, operating and capital gifts, endowment investment return, and other revenue sources, along with projections for each operating and capital cost center. Within each of these alternative futures, coverage (contribution) ratios describe the percentage of operating costs to be met by each element of the revenue stream. Thus, the endowment-support ratio describes the percentage of operating cost to be met by the component of endowment investment return applied to operations. The optimum value of the endowment-support ratio is determined within the framework of the totality of circumstances a school faces. It is that value prescribed by the most desirable future described within the strategic plan. In modeling alternative futures, the board considers the consequences of actions that would increase or decrease the ratio, providing larger or smaller levels of endowment support for operating needs. In the context of the totality of resources available and their allocations to cost centers, the board can subjectively judge the resulting utility of each model. Thus is the optimum value of the endowment-support ratio determined and the answer to the question, how much endowment is enough?

When additional endowment gifts are received, when large unrestricted gifts, bequests, or operating surpluses are added to the endowment, when enrollment, facilities or programs expand, or service levels for existing programs are increased (more output and/or increased outcomes), the strategic plan is modified accordingly, new futures are modeled, and a new optimum level for the endowment-support ratio is determined.

6

Knowledge Not Just for Knowledge's Sake

In terms of my profession, I'm passionate about financial literacy. I want to live in a financially literate society. I want kids to understand the importance of savings and investing. I want to try to replicate the great savers who came out of the Depression, the best savers the country has ever seen. It's crucial that people understand the importance of financial literacy, because it's actually life-saving.
—Mellody Hobson

Board knowledge is a key component to successful investing. The extent of mandated trustee training on investments varies across public plans, endowments, and trusts. Again, we can look to the corporate world for direction on the importance of trustee knowledge. For corporate boards, understanding financial statements was deemed so essential for public companies that the Sarbanes Oxley Act of 2002 mandated it for the audit committee of such organizations. Each company must disclose whether the committee possesses at least one "financial expert". That individual must have the following skills[1]:

- An understanding of financial statements and generally accepted accounting principles (GAAP)
- The ability to assess application of GAAP as it relates to accounting for estimates, accruals, and reserves

---

[1] "Sarbanes Oxley Audit Committee Requirements", Deloitte, 2004, p. 2.

© The Author(s) 2019
C. K. Merker, S. W. Peck, *The Trustee Governance Guide*,
https://doi.org/10.1007/978-3-030-21088-5_6

- Experience preparing, auditing, analyzing or evaluating financial statements or experience actively supervising those engaged in such activities
- An understanding of internal controls and procedures for financial reporting
- An understanding of audit committee functions

In our pension plan study, we found that the most effective organizations had high participation rates among both the audit and investment committees. To be effective, those organizations needed members who demonstrated both engagement and an adequate base of financial literacy.

However, the general lack of education to promote financial literacy is a significant and widespread problem and not just in the public pension plan world. In the "Retirement Income Literacy Survey" conducted for The American College of Financial Services in 2014, 80% of the respondents received scores of 60 or lower on financial questions about retirement. Just 20% received what amounted to a passing grade.[2]

The results are just as dismal when it comes to general financial knowledge. Asked five multiple-choice questions about topics like interest calculations, mortgage payments, and investments, just 39% of the 25,509 adults surveyed answered at least four correctly, according to a 2012 survey from the FINRA Investor Education Foundation.[3] That was down from 42% in 2009.

Many boards, as has been studied and documented, are held back by insufficient knowledge of its members. A 2001 UK government report, known as the Myners Report, concluded that a key problem area for pension funds is that "many trustees are not especially expert in investment".[4]

To illustrate this finding, the Report observed a majority of trustees had no professional qualifications in finance or investment, had little in the way of initial training, did not attend training courses after the first 12 months of appointment, and spent hardly any time in the course of a week preparing for pension fund investment decisions. Pension fund trustees may be well intentioned but there is no 'legal requirement for trustees to have any particular level of expertise in investment matters'.[5]

---

[2] https://retirement.theamericancollege.edu/research/ricp-retirement-income-literacy-survey

[3] http://www.usfinancialcapability.org

[4] Myners Report (2001), "Institutional Investment in the UK: a Review", HM Treasury, London.

[5] Clark, Gordon L., Caerlewy-Smith, Emiko, and Marshall, John C., "Pension Fund Competence: Decision Making in Problems Relevant to Investment Practice", Cambridge University Press, March, 2006, p. 4.

But how much financial literacy does any given board member need to be effective? To be literate, one must be in possession of certain skills. **Simple literacy** is the ability to read, and by that we mean on one level recognize symbols (grammar and syntax), but also have the capacity to interpret their meaning (definition and context). To be *numerate*, one must be able to read and understand quantities and their relationships. The National Financial Educators Council (NFEC) defines financial literacy as "possessing the skills and knowledge on financial matters to confidently take effective action that best fulfills an individual's personal, family and global community goals".[6]

Financial literacy, therefore, represents a combination of both literacy and numeracy within the context of financial issues, which for most would revolve around: (1) budgeting (planned saving and consumption), (2) use of credit (borrowing), and (3) investing (long-term saving). As a board member of an organization participating on a finance or investment committee, that person will be faced with issues that will require them to apply decisions, or at least monitor decisions, potentially across all three areas, taking the concept of financial literacy a step further into "financial competency".

A 2006 study of pension fund trustees by Clark, Caerlewy-Smith, and Marshall drilled down into the concept of pension fund trustee competency. The authors explained their reason for undertaking the study, noting that while there had been a significant amount of research done on individual decision-making in the behavioral finance field, there had been very few studies specific to trustee decision-making up to that point.

The study defined "consistent decision-making" as an indicator of trustee competency. Of that there are two kinds: that which is "competent", based upon pattern recognition and linked response, and that which is "expert", which is based upon substantive knowledge and deliberate decision technique.

Boards do not need to be manned by experts; they need only have competence. Expertise can be hired. However, good decisions must be made by boards in the face of uncertainty:

First, decision-making takes place under risk and uncertainty such that judgments are made amongst various probable outcomes (risk) and with recognition that there are unspecified events that may disrupt and change current circumstances (uncertainty). Second, strategic thinking is an important attribute of effective decision-making; being able to revise one's goals and switch from planned actions to other unanticipated courses of action could be just as important as long-term planning. Third, consistency in the application of effective techniques of decision-making rather than consistency of decisions with respect to given preferences may be the mark of expert decision-making.

---

[6] https://www.financialeducatorscouncil.org/financial-literacy-definition/

The study considered trustee problem-solving skills with investments and, in particular, what they described as "their discount functions", a concept we introduced in the prior section in the biases table. In other words, this meant their willingness to take risks with their own money and other people's money, their understanding of probability, and their efficiency in processing information.

The survey they applied was designed to examine widely recognized problems taken from the psychology literature and drew from many established tests and techniques. Four main conclusions from the experimental study found several shortcomings that suggest pension trustees are no better than members of the broader population in overcoming common cognitive biases as documented in the literature[7]:

1. Trustees generally have shallow and non-exponential discount functions. OK, stop there. What does this mean, "non-exponential discount functions"? Simply put, people do not look out into the future and mentally value what a given investment in today's dollars might be worth in the future, given the potential for risk, by discounting the value, and estimating an implied required rate of return.

This skill is important for making choices, among a wide range of investments, or classes of investments (asset class), that may have differences in liquidity, time horizon, and volatility. As a group, it was nearly impossible to define a simple function, which meant that people were all over the board in terms of their individual estimates. Trustees did not evaluate consistently the **time value of money** within the context of inherent conditions of uncertainty and risk. Time value of money is the idea that money will have a value worth more or less in the future, either through the erosive effects of inflation or the compounding effects of interest (reinvestment).

2. Trustees in general responded that they would assume a moderate amount of risk. However, in measuring implicit risk preferences, it was found that individuals are risk and **loss averse**. Now stop there again. What is risk and loss aversion?

In cognitive psychology and decision theory, loss aversion refers to people's tendency to prefer avoiding losses to acquiring equivalent gains; for example, it is better to not lose $5 than to find $5. What distinguishes loss aversion from risk aversion is that the utility of a monetary payoff depends on what

---

[7] Ibid., p. 22.

was previously experienced or was expected to happen. Some studies have suggested that losses are twice as powerful, psychologically, as gains.[8]

In marketing, the use of trial periods and rebates tries to take advantage of the buyer's tendency to value the good more after the buyer incorporates it in the status quo. In general, from past behavioral economics studies, people will participate with uncertain payoffs until the threat of loss equals any incurred gains.

What is interesting about loss aversion, in contrast to risk aversion, is that a strong preference to avoid losses can morph into **risk-seeking behavior**. Good examples of this would be so-called rogue traders like Nick Leeson, the 1990s trader who lost $2 billion dollars while working at Baring's Bank in the Far East. As losses became greater and greater, Leeson took on more risky bets with the bank's money, until the losses became exponential, bringing the bank to the brink of default until it was acquired by ING.[9] Table 6.1 summarizes these concepts in terms of the fourfold pattern in prospect theory: how the prospect of a loss or gain changes behavior under varying conditions of certain and possible outcomes.

Evolutionary psychology leads to further application of this concept into explaining what has become known as the **endowment effect**. Humans may be hardwired to be loss averse due to asymmetric evolutionary pressure on

Table 6.1 Prospect theory: the fourfold pattern

	Gains	Losses
High probability certainty effect	95% chance to win $10,000 (100% to win $1000) Fear of disappointment RISK AVERSE Accept unfavorable settlement (e.g. legal settlements)	95% chance to lose $10,000 (100% to lose $1000) Hope to avoid loss RISK SEEKING Reject favorable settlement (e.g. rogue traders)
Low probability possibility effect	5% chance to win $10,000 (95% chance of $0) Hope of large gain RISK SEEKING Reject favorable settlement (e.g. lotteries)	5% chance to lose $10,000 (95% chance of $0) Fear of large loss RISK AVERSE Accept unfavorable settlement (e.g. insurance)

Kahnemann, Daniel, *Thinking Fast and Slow*, Farrar, Straus and Giroux, pp. 317–318

---

[8] Kahneman, D. & Tversky, A. (1992). "Advances in prospect theory: Cumulative representation of uncertainty". *Journal of Risk and Uncertainty* 5 (4): 297–323.
[9] Leeson, Nick, *Rogue Trader: How I Brought Down Barings Bank and Shook the Financial World*, Sphere, 1996.

losses and gains: for an organism operating close to the edge of survival, the loss of a day's food could cause death, whereas the gain of an extra day's food would not cause an extra day of life (unless the food could be easily and effectively stored).

3. Trustees are ill-equipped to make **probability estimates**. Without training, people do not typically understand the steps necessary for calculating probabilities. In making rough probability judgments, people commonly depend upon one of several simplified rules of thumb that greatly ease the burden of decision.

Using the **availability rule**, people judge the probability of an event by the ease with which they can imagine relevant instances of similar events or the number of such events that they can easily remember. The problem is, that if they are unfamiliar with the item for which they are making forecasts, they may form no judgment at all or at most make a simple guess. In the context of group decision-making, they may simply bow out from any decision whatsoever and go with the flow on the group decision.

With the **anchoring strategy**, people pick some natural starting point for a first approximation and then adjust this figure based on the results of additional information or analysis. Typically, they do not adjust the initial judgment enough.

4. Finally, trustees are subject to **confirmation bias**, selecting information to confirm presuppositions, and do not use available data efficiently to test solutions to problems.

Belief persistence and confirmation bias can disrupt the process that boards need to follow in making decisions and not fall prey to **hindsight bias**, which causes boards to, as we mentioned earlier, to "chase the hot dot" by sticking with losers and avoiding winners.

These findings were further corroborated by our own work. We found that the most effectively governed boards not only had high engagement by board members with the investment and audit process, but also had high participation from both internal staff and the external consultant. The reason: because these individuals were best placed to advise the trustees on investment decisions and provide that layer of "expert competency". In the final analysis, it is not necessary for board trustees to be experts on their own, but they do need to then surround themselves with a group of experts.

7

Origins of Financial Illiteracy

Is financial literacy important to competent board decision-making? The short answer is, of course, yes. There are many and frequent trustee educational conferences to help trustees make informed decisions. But in Sarah's experience in attending these conferences, many attendees often felt overwhelmed and embarrassed by their lack of investment knowledge. They should not be. Financial illiteracy is widespread and seen everywhere in the US, whether it's the low savings rates among aggregate American households, chronically underfunded state and municipal pension systems, or even the federal government's ongoing tolerance for large budget deficits even in good times, when tax receipts are higher, and public funding needs are less (i.e., for unemployment insurance). Beyond effective board governance, the implications are severe for a society whose citizenry cannot function effectively when making decisions about credit, consumption, saving, and investing.

In the book *The Missing Semester*, the authors discuss what should have been covered as children come up through our educational system—financial literacy training.[1] While certain noncore subjects besides reading, writing, and arithmetic include courses like civics, there has been no emphasis to provide a course to equip children with the essential skills to handle household budgeting, management of credit, and the basics of saving and investing for education and retirement.

The impact of not training our citizenry to be financially literate is reflected in how households deal with their finances. A review of the statistics is shocking. According to a recent study by the Global Financial Literacy

---

[1] Natali, Gene and Kabala, Matt, *The Missing Semester*, self-published, 2012.

© The Author(s) 2019
C. K. Merker, S. W. Peck, *The Trustee Governance Guide*,
https://doi.org/10.1007/978-3-030-21088-5_7

Excellence Center, one in three Americans are unable to cope with unexpected expenses.[2] Additionally, only 44% of US workers participate in a corporate-defined contribution plan. An unbelievable half of the workers in the US are not saving for retirement at all.[3]

When testing financial literacy knowledge itself, only 13% of people aged 18–24 can correctly answer three key financial literacy questions. That number only jumps to 24% for people aged 30–34. And less than a third of Americans know basic financial concepts by age 40, even though most important household financial decisions are made well before that age.[4] Those who demonstrate financial literacy are more likely to[5]:

- have precautionary savings,
- have planned for retirement,
- have financial investments beyond retirement accounts, and
- be current on credit card and loan payments.

Perhaps the global financial crisis in 2008 could have been less severe had people been equipped with basic financial literacy skills. For one, despite the free availability of credit, they would have been able to assess the purchase price of a home in relation to their annual income and made a more informed decision about whether to purchase that first, or in many cases second, home. Or perhaps they would not have taken on mortgages that were both complex and sounded too good to be true, yet, let them finally purchase their "dream house". That point of purchase decision opened the gate to what eventually became a frenzied housing bubble. If people had understood what they were buying, this may have stopped the mania before it had even started.

So, back to the question: why isn't the US population financially literate? This is where we depart from empirical data, and speculate, and it starts with the so-called Silent Generation, the generation that followed the group known as the "Greatest Generation" that survived the Great Depression and fought in at least one world war, and possibly two, and preceded the "Baby Boom" generation. For that generation talking about money wasn't polite conversation, and it was information to be treated with the highest confidentiality and respect.

---

[2] "Financial Fragility in the U.S.: Evidence and Implications", by Andrea Hasler, Annamaria Lusardi, Noemi Oggero, Global Financial Literacy Excellence Center, The George Washington University School of Business", April 2018.
[3] Merker, Christopher K. *Asset Owner Governance and Fiduciary Effectiveness: The Case of Public Pensions*, Marquette University, May 2017.
[4] http://gflec.org/wp-content/uploads/2018/02/GFLEC-Empowering-Youth-Fact-Sheet.pdf?x87657
[5] TIAA Institute – GFLEC Personal Finance Index.

Further, there were limits on consumer credit and credit terms were simpler. Fixed rate mortgages were the convention, and more exotic type of mortgages that became prevalent during the run up to the great financial crisis of 2008 were unheard of.

In addition to money matters being a generally taboo subject, there was something else driving a general lack of interest around financial education: the establishment of social safety nets in response to the suffering during the Great Depression along with the postwar economic boom. Leading up to and for about half a century after, we saw the development and expansion of the social "safety net" and subsidy-type state interventions in fundamental aspects of economic life for the country, including education, retirement savings, mortgage finance, health care insurance, and, when things become really bad, like during the Great Depression, food security and employment.

We also witnessed a golden age period in US history, sometimes referred in economics as "the Long Boom" or the "Golden Age of Capitalism", the post–World War II period. During this time, the US became a global hegemon in the aftermath of the war, rebuilding Europe and the Far East. From 1950 to 1973, the US economy expanded at a brisk annualized GDP growth rate of 4.8%.[6]

While this was a truly a remarkable period in US history, and despite being a relatively short period of time in the grand scheme of things, the impacts are still being felt today in the way people feel and think about their, for lack of a better phrase, economic security. During this time and some years prior to it, people were born, most received a high school education, a few went on to college, they then went to work at the local factory or as a teacher, held that same job for 40 years, earned a high enough wage to more than make ends meet, enough to buy a house and a family car, and along with Social Security enjoyed both a corporate or public pension at retirement, and then didn't live long enough to run the risk of running out of money.

So, what training did people need for managing their money? Cash flow was reliable, jobs were secure, housing was plentiful and affordable, and health and retirement security were guaranteed. People did not need to make complex financial decisions and as a result did not need financial education to make them. And for those that lived through the Depression, they were also incredible savers.

That picture began to change with the baby boomers in the 1970s. It was called deindustrialization. In addition to people becoming, over a period of years, hyper-consumers during what also became known as the Golden Age of

---

[6] Skidelsky, Robert (2009). *Keynes: The Return of the Master*. Allen Lane. pp. 116, 126.

Advertising—buying up everything in sight—suddenly and at the same time, the underpinnings of our financial security began to erode. Jobs shifted to lower-wage countries, wages began to stagnate, people went through periods of unemployment, inflation began to take hold both in healthcare and in education, unions no longer had power over collective bargaining, and that pension plan everyone expected to cover the costs of retirement suddenly was frozen or shut down. What was left converted to a voluntary defined contribution plan, 401(k) or 403(b), where the employee now had to fund retirement with a portion of their own wages and make their own investment decisions.

Talk about a change! Almost overnight we went from a generation that had little to worry about, to a generation that had everything to worry about, and financial success suddenly hinged, not just on your education level and job skills, but also on your ability to manage your own money effectively. The delayed reaction to this shift has been equally striking.

We are only now, late in the second decade of the twenty-first century, and more than 45 years after the beginning of the Great Stagflation, seeing financial literacy on the docket of state legislatures. A handful of states have already enacted mandatory financial literacy at the high school level, such as in Wisconsin and Illinois, which only passed in 2017. However, in 2018 this appears to have reached a crescendo with 29 states and Puerto Rico all pursuing some form of financial literacy legislation.[7]

Does financial literacy improve financial outcomes? Yes. For example, here in southeastern Wisconsin, an organization that was formed over a decade ago, SecureFutures, started with the idea of bringing financial literacy into the classroom, taught by financial professionals, using a condensed curriculum over a three-week period. It is targeted at teens aged 16–17, who are ripe for this type of education. Many are at the stage they may be first earning money from a part-time job, facing expenses from using a car, and so on.

Since that program started, it is now taught in over 100 high schools, colleges, and technical colleges, in many socioeconomically diverse communities. During that decade plus, over 70,000 students have received training, and the organization has been around long enough they can track the results of this targeted effort. Figure 7.1 shows some of the pre- and post-results from the program. Recently, they have developed a module, Money Path, that focuses on budgeting and financial planning for early college level based on potential career choices and borrowing for education.

---

[7] National Conference of State Legislatures http://www.ncsl.org/research/financial-services-and-commerce/financial-literacy-2018-legislation.aspx

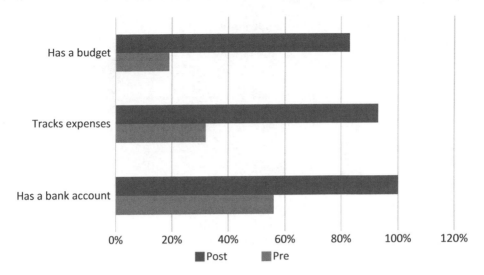

Fig. 7.1 How money coach improved student financial behavior. (Source: SecureFutures)

We make these points about financial literacy for the overall population because we believe they have strong implications for the importance of financial literacy for board members. For the 1.6% of the population that make up the fiduciaries and trustees responsible for 80% of the investments made in the US across the many pensions, endowments, and foundations, these people must have the sufficient skills and diligence to at a minimum find and retain the expertise around them to be most effective.[8] See Fig. 7.2 for a graph on the number of institutions and assets by organization type in the US.

To conclude this section, some basic and essential advice from Benjamin Franklin, who, in *The Art of Making Money Plenty*, arguably the first book on financial literacy, said:

> At this time when the general complaint is that money is so scarce it must be an act of kindness to instruct the moneyless how they can reinforce their pockets. I will acquaint all with the true secret of money catching, the certain way to fill empty purses and how to keep them always full.
>
> Two simple rules well observed will do the business. First, let honesty and hard work be thy constant companions; Second, spend one cent less every day than they clearly gain. Then shall thy pockets soon begin to thrive, thy creditors will never

---

[8] Merker, Christopher Kinne, "Asset Owner Governance and Fiduciary Effectiveness: The Case of Public Pension Plans" (2017). *Dissertations (2009 -)*. 713, http://epublications.marquette.edu/dissertations_mu/713, p. 22.

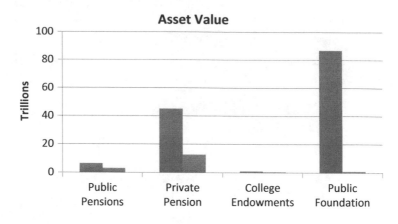

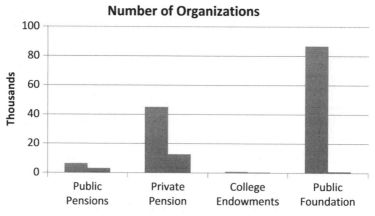

Fig. 7.2 Asset ownership in the US. (Merker, Christopher Kinne, "Asset Owner Governance and Fiduciary Effectiveness: The Case of Public Pension Plans" (2017). *Dissertations (2009 -).* 713, http://epublications.marquette.edu/dissertations_mu/713, p. 21)

insult thee, nor want oppress, nor hunger bite, nor nakedness freeze thee; the whole hemisphere will shine brighter and pleasure spring up in every corner of thy heart. Thereby embrace these rules and be happy.

Practitioner Focus: Investment 101 and Foundation Board Basics

Investment 101

It is not necessary to go back to school to purse an advanced degree to obtain a reasonable degree of financial literacy as a board member or trustee of an organization with a dedicated investment fund. One of the only programs of its kind out there, a relatively new program, is offered by the CFA Institute, and it is free. It is called the **Investment Foundation's Program**, and further information about it may be found at https://www.cfainstitute.org/en/programs/investment-foundations.

The program covers the essentials of finance, ethics, and investment roles, and provides an overview of the global investment industry. This self-study program is designed for disciplines outside of investment roles, those who work alongside those responsible for investing, and provides a great knowledge base for board trustees. It covers concepts, industry structure, ethics and regulation, performance evaluation and risk management. There is no education or experience requirement, and the optional online exam is offered at test centers around the world to receive the program certificate.

There are also a number of training programs specifically geared to trustee education, such as the **Commonfund Investment Stewardship Academy**, https://www.commonfund.org/commonfund-institute/. The program offers "an immersion in the essential principles and practices of managing long-term and perpetual capital". Over a four-day workshop at Yale, participants learn how to address the investment challenges their organizations face. It offers a foundational education in policy, portfolios, and processes and practical experience via a simulated committee meeting. Another organization involved in ongoing trustee education is the **International Foundation of Employee Benefit Plans**, https://www.ifebp.org, which conducts educational workshops year-round. Its emphasis is on the trustees and staff of public pensions, multi-employer plans and corporate retirement programs.

Foundation Board Basics[9]

BoardSource, a nonprofit organization, dedicated to serving the needs of nonprofits and foundations, also provides an essential knowledge framework for foundation board members:

Foundation Tax Rules

The IRS has registered nearly 80,000 private foundations. The Tax Reform Act of 1969 created the concept and legal framework for foundations as we know them today. The purpose of this law was to prevent private exploitation of charitable trusts and foundations. There are two key elements of the law: (1) It stipulated a minimum payout rate at 6% (since then lowered to 5%), and (2) it forbade self-dealing—business transactions with board members. Foundations

---

[9] https://boardsource.org/resources/foundation-board-basics/ Reprinted with permission.

also need to pay an excise tax on their net investment income and must not earmark grants for lobbying, possess more than 20% of business holdings in any single business, and engage in risky investments.

Donor Intent

Usually one or several major contributions—or money transfers—create the endowment of a foundation. During this transfer, the donor delegates the overall management and supervision of the funds to the foundation's board and stipulates the primary objectives of their use. The board has a foremost duty to respect the original intent of the donor. In a way, the donor creates the original mission for the foundation and may indicate the types of activities that the foundation will support. It is worth repeating, nonetheless, that the donor gives up the "ownership" of the funds—he or she alone can no longer make financial decisions regarding the use of the funds or control the details of grant making. Without this premise, the original gift is not tax deductible.

Building a Board

The composition of foundation boards varies greatly depending on who creates the organization. Corporate foundation boards mostly consist of company executives and other senior employees to ensure alignment with the company's priorities.

Family foundation board members usually include the donor (if still alive) and other family members to ensure that the donor intent is respected—or properly interpreted if detailed guidelines no longer exist or have become outdated.

Independent foundations often have more "outsiders" on their boards. The original board usually reflects the preferences of the founder, but with time, as the founder connection weakens, the composition of the board evolves. These foundation boards tend to include individuals who are interested in the mission area of the organization and who bring specific expertise with them.

It is commonly accepted that "insiders"—relatives, friends, or business colleagues—may serve on a foundation board. However, even under these circumstances, onboarding members who have no personal or business relationship with the foundation makes ample sense. An outsider perspective or expertise that otherwise is not included generally allows the board to widen its point of view, to better scrutinize its decisions, and to better reflect the needs of the grantees.

Self-Dealing

All nonprofits must steer away from private inurement—offering insiders financial benefits that are greater than what they provide in return. Rules are even stricter for foundation board members. No trustee may participate in a financial transaction as the provider and receiver of the benefit. In practice, this means that no trustee may, for example, engage in buying, selling, or leasing property with the foundation; borrow money from the foundation; or lend interest-bearing funds. It is acceptable, however, to pay for a member's professional (legal, accounting, investment management) services.

Compensation

Compensating foundation board members for their governance work is not considered self-dealing, as long as the pay is reasonable. It is worth noting, however, that due to some bad practices, foundations have received unwanted publicity concerning compensation that clearly misused foundation assets to benefit its trustees and managers. Most nonprofit board members serve as volunteers, and the preferable approach is to separate governance work and paid staff activities. If foundation trustees wear multiple hats and hiring staff is not feasible, it may be appropriate and is legal to discuss compensation, however.

Grant Making

Private foundations are required by law to distribute at least 5% of their net investment assets on an annual basis. The purpose of this law is to eliminate excessive hoarding of assets and to make foundations respect their primary mandate: granting funds to eligible charities and thus benefiting society.

An ongoing debate vacillates between the actual payout percentage and the types of expenses that can be included in the calculations. If a foundation is to exist in perpetuity, it wants to make sure that inflation and other unavoidable expenses do not erode its endowment. Some question whether 5% is the right figure; others focus on the need to do more. Some question whether certain administrative expenses should continue to be included in the calculations or be absorbed separately. The board's role here is to set the tone and determine the values for the foundation.

Assessment of Impact

Increasingly, foundations state expectations for their grantees. They set performance standards, want to track how the grant money is spent, and expect measurable positive results. Via reports and site visits, they want to see the impact their grants make. Today, many foundations are including themselves in this scrutiny. By requiring self-assessment and studying the foundation's own performance, these foundation boards are serving as an example to their grantees.

Private foundations are privileged charitable organizations: Due to their endowments, they usually do not need to raise funds, but rather are in the business of distributing money to other charities and those in need. The primary duty of the foundation board, as is true for all nonprofit boards, is to remain loyal to its stated mission and priorities.

Part III

The Third Imperative: *Be Diversified*

8

30,000 Products

Diversification as a foundational principle for investing is commonly accepted and understood today, and it is a concept that is really taken for granted. However, there is a long history associated with diversification that evolved over time through the development of trade and the application of mathematics to provide such underpinnings, which addressed some very real world problems. Harry Markowitz once said:

A good portfolio is more than a long list of good stocks and bonds. It is a balanced whole, providing the investor with protections and opportunities with respect to a wide range of contingencies.

Diversification, as a principle of risk reduction, is an old concept. To attach a date to it, we would have to go back several hundred years in history. For today's modern board, however, it is a must, and is next on our list of imperatives. However, the challenge in today's world is not whether to diversify but rather where to stop with it. Options for portfolio selection are almost limitless, and certainly not all options are of equal value or merit.

There are approximately 100,000 publicly traded stocks globally, and a similar number of corporate bonds. In the sovereign and municipal fixed-income universe, there are over one million unique issues trading in the market. And, of course, the mutual funds, exchange-traded funds (ETFs), and hedge funds that slice and dice, and re-slice and re-dice this group of stocks and bonds are in excess of 30,000 products. And just like restaurants in New York City, there are dozens opening and closing every day.

© The Author(s) 2019
C. K. Merker, S. W. Peck, *The Trustee Governance Guide*,
https://doi.org/10.1007/978-3-030-21088-5_8

You can own each piece of the market in numerous different ways, as part of a sector, an index, or an index sector, an active portfolio, as part of a hedged strategy, and so on. You can go long or short on investments, or you can invest in a trading strategy that seeks to profit from inefficiencies in the market, such as in a global macro or long-short strategy, which may combine both approaches.

You can own directly real assets such as real estate, commodities, and currencies. Or you can invest indirectly in related derivative securities (options, futures, forwards, and swaps). You can own them indirectly as well in the form of a limited partnership, mutual fund, or exchange traded note (ETN).[1] You can also invest in partnerships that own private equity and hedge funds. And there are new classes of investments that come around every few years, such as we are seeing with the rise of environmental, social, and governance (ESG) and other "sustainable" investments, and with the cryptocurrencies like Bitcoin and Ethereum, which we will cover in the practitioner section at the end of this chapter.

We believe that understanding the history of diversification is instructive for trustees and can be helpful for understanding the role that diversification plays in executing a trustee's fiduciary duty. The discussion of cryptocurrencies is an example of the pitfalls of chasing a new product and, again, can provide a valuable lesson for how trustees should think about diversification.

Some History

The Medicis in Italy, circa 1397, were among the first to apply the technique of diversification successfully on a large commercial scale. In their case, the problem they addressed was the difficulty and risk of moving and paying for commodities across the Mediterranean trade routes. Individually, both buyer and seller were at risk on any given transaction. A bank, such as the one the Medicis owned, could help in such cases by stepping in to guarantee the transaction through the use of an instrument called a Banker's Acceptance. This financial innovation has had staying power: To this day due to their perceived safety, banker's acceptances are regularly used as financial instruments in international trade dealings.

A banker's acceptance allows companies dealing overseas to complete transactions without the need to extend credit. An importing business can issue a

---

[1] An ETN is like an ETF, but a debt instrument, instead of an equity instrument. For example, the Alerian Master Limited Partnership (MLP) index fund is an ETN (ALN). The underlying assets are pipeline companies owned through partnerships, but the ETN passes on the income of the underlying holdings. MLPs are notorious for requiring K-1 tax reporting in every state in which there is a partnership, and most cross numerous states. Through this structure there are conveniently no K-1 s, because nothing is truly owned in the form of equity; the investment is, in effect, loaned money.

banker's acceptance with a date beyond when a shipment is expected to be delivered, and the exporting business can have a payment instrument in hand before finalizing a shipment.

For the Medicis, the widespread use of banker's acceptances allowed them to mitigate the unique risk of any single transaction to the bank under the Law of Large Numbers.[2] *The Medicis diversified their risk by underwriting hundreds and thousands of such transactions.* Also, the Medici banker, as transaction facilitator, could appropriately price, via the commission or spread on the transaction, to further reduce the potential loss on any given transaction.

A later—but still early—application of this technique was in the form of the world's first joint-stock company, the Dutch East India Company (the Vereenigde Oost-Indische Compagnie, or simply, VOC). In this case the risk was the merchant vessel to the Far East Indies, a long and dangerous journey around the Cape of Good Hope. The failure rate of nonreturning merchant vessels was something in the order of 40%, but the profit from those that made it could be as high as four times the initial investment. The creation of the VOC allowed diversification on a massive scale across merchant vessels; at its peak the company owned as many as 5000 ships:

> Before the establishment of the VOC in 1602, individual ships were funded by merchants as limited partnerships that ceased to exist when the ships returned.
>
> Merchants would invest in several ships at a time so that if one failed to return, they weren't wiped out. The establishment of the VOC allowed hundreds of ships to be funded simultaneously by hundreds of investors to minimize risk.[3]

As a sidenote, the VOC to this day, on an inflation-adjusted basis, is the largest, most successful, and longest-running public company in world history (1602–1800), even compared to the modern behemoths like Amazon and Berkshire Hathaway.[4] Not bad for humanity's first run at creating a public company.

---

[2] In probability theory, the law of large numbers (LLN) is a theorem that describes the result of performing the same experiment a large number of times. According to the law, the average of the results obtained from a large number of trials should be close to the expected value, and will tend to become closer as more trials are performed. The LLN is important because it guarantees stable long-term results for the averages of some random events. For example, while a casino may lose money in a single spin of the roulette wheel, its earnings will tend toward a predictable percentage over a large number of spins. Any winning streak by a player will eventually be overcome by the parameters of the game. It is important to remember that the law only applies (as the name indicates) when a large number of observations are considered. There is no principle that a small number of observations will coincide with the expected value or that a streak of one value will immediately be "balanced" by the others (e.g., gambler's fallacy).

[3] http://www.businessinsider.com/rise-and-fall-of-united-east-india-2013-11

[4] Planes, Alex, "A History of Ridiculously Big Companies: Apple takes its place in the pantheon of capitalism", Aug 22, 2012, motleyfool.com

More Recently

The first diversified pool of funds, of course, also was developed by the Dutch, who were responsible for so many of the innovations in modern finance, including that first public company. In response to the financial crisis of 1772–1773, Amsterdam-based businessman Adriaan van Ketwich formed a trust named Eendragt Maakt Magt ("unity creates strength"). His aim was to provide small investors with an opportunity to diversify.[5]

One historical note on the financial crisis of that period, which was credit-driven in nature and affected much of Europe, it also impacted the fledgling 13 British colonies in North America that were on the cusp of becoming the United States. With some historical irony, the VOC was also involved here; and it essentially set off a chain of events that lead to the tax on tea, further straining relations between the colonies and Great Britain and resulted in the Boston Tea Party of 1773, a precursor event, of course, to the American Revolution.[6]

Much later, mutual funds were introduced in the US in the 1890s. Early US funds were generally closed-end funds with a fixed number of shares that often traded at prices above or below the portfolio net asset value. The first open-end mutual fund with redeemable shares was established on March 21, 1924, as the Massachusetts Investors Trust. It is still in existence today and is now managed by MFS Investment Management.

In the US, closed-end funds remained more popular than open-end funds throughout the 1920s. In 1929, open-end funds accounted for only 5% of the industry's $27 billion in total assets. This all changed as the result of the Great Depression, as rules tightened to protect investors:

---

[5] Goetzmann, William N.; Rouwenhorst, K. Geert (2005). *The Origins of Value: The Financial Innovations that Created Modern Capital Markets.*

[6] The crisis set off a chain of events related to the controversy over the colonial tea market. The Dutch East India Company was one of the firms that suffered the hardest hits in the crisis. Failing to pay or renew its loan from the Bank of England, the firm sought to sell its 18 million pounds of tea from its British ware-houses to the American colonies. Back then, the firm had to market its tea to the colonies through middlemen, so the high price made its tea unfavorable compared to the tea that was smuggled in or was produced locally in the colonies. In May 1773, however, the Parliament imposed a three pence tax for each pound of tea sold and allowed the firm for the first time to sell directly through its own agents. The Tea Act reduced the tea price and solidified the East India Company's monopoly over the local tea business in the colonial tea market. Furious about how British government and the East India Company controlled the colonial tea trade, citizens in Charleston, Philadelphia, New York, and Boston rejected the imported tea, and these protests eventually led to the Boston Tea Party in 1773.

1. The Securities Act of 1933 required that all investments sold to the public, including mutual funds, be registered with the Securities and Exchange Commission (SEC) and that they provide prospective investors with a prospectus that discloses essential facts about the investment.
2. The Securities and Exchange Act of 1934 required that issuers of securities, including mutual funds, report regularly to their investors; this act also created the SEC, which is the principal regulator of mutual funds.
3. The Revenue Act of 1936 established guidelines for the taxation of mutual funds.
4. The Investment Company Act of 1940 established rules specifically governing mutual funds, and in particular was interpreted by the Supreme Court as instilling a fiduciary duty on investment managers, despite the fact, that the word is never once used in the legislation.

Once rules were in place, the flexible nature of the open-ended mutual fund, with daily liquidity where investors could contribute money or redeem shares at the stated end of the trading day Net Asset Value (NAV), was simply more attractive than a closed-end fund that was usually priced above or below its underlying holdings, and had more limited liquidity.

Practitioner Focus: Cryptocurrencies

Speaking of rules to protect investors, let us talk about the cryptos. What are cryptocurrencies, and, more to the point, should I be diversifying into them? The first thing to know about cryptos is a technology called "blockchain".

A blockchain is a digitized, decentralized, public ledger of transactions. Constantly growing as "completed" blocks, the most recent transactions are recorded and added to it in chronological order. It allows market participants to keep track of digital financial transactions without central recordkeeping. Each node, which is a computer connected to the network, gets a copy of the blockchain downloaded automatically.

Originally developed as the accounting method for the virtual currency, Bitcoin, blockchains are appearing in a variety of commercial applications today. Currently, the technology is primarily used to verify transactions, and within digital currencies, it is possible to digitize, code, and insert practically any document into the blockchain. Doing so creates an indelible record that cannot be changed; and furthermore, the record's authenticity can be verified by the entire community using the blockchain, instead of a single centralized authority.

So, a digital currency is a security that works on the basis of blockchain. The process of verifying and adding to the digital transaction records is called "mining". There are many such currencies with Bitcoin, Ethereum, and Litecoin among the best known. An investor in Bitcoin goes to a provider such as Coin Base (www.coinbase.com) and converts real currency to Bitcoin. The investor then has an account online containing the issuance that can then be transacted with other participants in that market. Some participants accept it as "legal" tender, while others simply hold the currency as an investment.

What's not to like about a currency that is secure, unalterable, not subject to counterfeit, and has immediate settlement?

To understand the shortcomings, one must understand the inherent characteristics of any successful currency. For it to have utility, there are three "must haves": (1) it must be a store of value; (2) it must be a medium of exchange; and (3) it must be a unit of account.

There are other qualities that improve the quality of any given currency, including general acceptability, portability, durability, homogeneity, cognizability, and stability of value, but these are extras. The main qualities are the three points noted above.[7] Now, let us consider each for cryptocurrencies:

1. **Store of value**: The first problem with cryptos is their value is highly turbulent and speculative. In 2017, we saw a bubble emerge and burst in the asset class with Bitcoin's value at one point reaching nearly $20,000 per unit. See Fig. 8.1 for a chart on the impressive growth and collapse of Bitcoin. Today, Bitcoin is trading around $5000 per unit, nearly 75% below its peak, and ranks first among the largest and most rapid investment bubbles in history since, and including, the Dutch Tulip Bubble of the 16th century.

For a currency to be useful on a broad scale, it is important for its value to be stable. First, it is unlikely for a currency to be adopted without this condition present. Secondly, assuming this first condition is overcome, and widespread adoption of cryptos occurs, time after time throughout history, currencies that are highly unstable—what in economics is referred to as highly inflationary or deflationary currencies—tend to be short-lived, and end up being replaced with something else: either a more stable foreign currency as we have seen in parts of Latin American (time and time again), where the US dollar has at different times been adopted as the replacement currency, or a new domestic currency replaces the old currency altogether.

---

[7] Singh, J. "Top 8 Qualities of an Ideal Money Material" http://www.economicsdiscussion.net/money/top-8-qualities-of-an-ideal-money-material/609

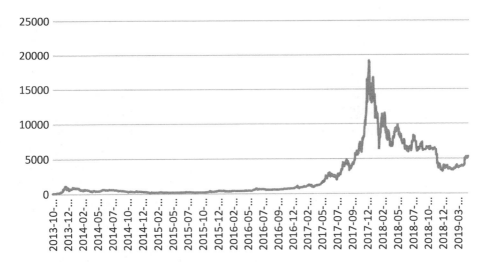

Fig. 8.1 Bitcoin, rise and fall

The second problem with cryptos, paradoxically, is both its widespread availability and limited supply. On its face, it sounds like a contradiction in terms, so let us take each characteristic in turn. (i) **Widespread availability**: today there are literally dozens of competing cryptos. Granted there are a couple that are leading the pack, but the problem is there are simply too many competing for the same "wallet share", and there are few barriers to entry. (ii) **Limited supply**: for those that become more established—and perhaps that happens and we see one or two dominate—the next problem is that sooner or later the "miner's" reach a point of diminishing returns in terms of what they can create given the constraints of the technology; there are only so many Bitcoins that can be mined or minted. By the way, it was the limits of supply that initially attracted investors: great for an investor, but not so helpful for buyer and seller. For a currency to be successful it needs to grow and flex— without constraint—to keep pace with economic expansion and contraction, something that a government regulator, like a central bank, is set up to manage and oversee.

2. **Medium of exchange**: Yes, we have heard the stories of people purchasing condos with Bitcoin, but the fact is, most merchants do not accept cryptos. Until there is widespread acceptance for the purpose of transacting in the real economy, there will not be much utility.
3. **Unit of account**: Here, cryptos check the box, but that is simply numbers on the page, and no different from other predominant forms of money.

What about the application of blockchain to credit card transactions? Wouldn't a blockchain enable greater security around such financial activity? In concept, yes, but here we run into another technological obstacle: blockchain is extremely energy intensive and slow to process. There are literally millions of credit card transactions happening every hour, and at the current state of the art, blockchain can only process a fraction of that volume. It also consumes enormous amounts of energy. Someday, these issues may be overcome through innovation in computer processing speeds, but today, again, given the current constraints of blockchain technology, it is totally unfit for credit card systems.

Our discussion about limitations in computer processing power in this book could be immediately proven wrong as soon as this book is in print. But here are the facts on developments in computing power: While for years Moore's law seemed to be firmly in place with the exponential growth in computer processing speeds, that trend has diminished in recent years.[8]

The chip industry has kept Moore's prediction alive, with Intel leading the charge. And computing companies have found plenty to do with the continual supply of extra transistors. But Intel pushed back its next transistor technology, with features as small as 10 nanometers, from 2016 to late 2017. The company has also decided to increase the time between future generations (see "Intel Puts the Brakes on Moore's Law"). And a technology roadmap for Moore's Law maintained by an industry group, including the world's largest chip makers, is being scrapped. Intel has suggested silicon transistors can only keep shrinking for another five years.[9]

More recently, since the above excerpt from the MIT article that appeared back in 2016, the current trend is that we will see about 10% increases in processing power over the next five years: not nearly the 500% increase of prior years over a similar time period. Every so often a computer science research project comes along with great hopes of a breakthrough, but so far nothing has come of it. We are not saying it will not happen, but it is likely to be some time before we see a transformation in this area to the point of supporting widespread blockchain application to things that require huge amounts of processing power to move quickly enough, like credit card processing.

---

[8] Moore's law is named after Intel cofounder Gordon Moore. He observed in 1965 that transistors were shrinking so fast that every year twice as many could fit onto a chip, and in 1975 adjusted the pace to a doubling every two years.

[9] Simonite, Tom, "Moore's Law is Dead: Now What?", *MIT Technology Review*, May 13, 2016.

So, what about when applied to financial securities? This brings up the related concept of the initial coin offering, or ICO. Blockchain technology applied to stocks and bonds is, indeed, a novel idea. Application to today's system of securities registration and trading across multiple platforms and systems could enhance both the security and efficiency of such transactions. However, the unregulated presence of ICOs has already been subject to fraud and abuse, and the SEC is moving rapidly to catch up on this with new regulation that will bring ICOs into the fold of normalized securities regulation with registration, disclosure, and other investor protections just like any other financial security.

A study that came out in July 2018, prepared by ICO advisory firm Statis Group, revealed that more than 80% of initial coin offerings (ICOs) conducted in 2017 were identified as scams.[10] The study took into consideration the lifecycle of ICOs run in 2017, from the initial proposal of a sale to the most mature phase of trading on a crypto exchange.

The research says that in 2017 "over 70 percent of ICO funding (by dollar volume) to-date went to higher quality projects, although over 80 percent of projects (by number share) were identified as scams. The analysts found that four percent of ICOs failed, and three percent had 'gone dead'. The study defined ICO death as 'not listed on exchanges for trading and has not had a code contribution in Github on a rolling three-month basis from that point in time'".

According to the study, total funding of coins and tokens in 2017 amounted to $11.9 billion. $1.34 billion (11%) of ICO funding went to scams. This suggests that while a large number of ICOs were scams, they received very little funding when compared with the industry as a whole.

The SEC has commented on their website that "companies and individuals are increasingly considering initial coin offerings (ICOs) as a way to raise capital or participate in investment opportunities. While these digital assets and the technology behind them may present a new and efficient means for carrying out financial transactions, they also bring increased risk of fraud and manipulation because the markets for these assets are less regulated than traditional capital markets". The likelihood, given recent court rulings, is that the area will eventually be classified as securities, and regulations will harmonize around these offerings in the same way as they do for traditional stocks, bonds, exchanges, and broker/dealers.

---

[10] Alexandre, Ana, "New Study Says 80 Percent of ICOs Conducted in 2017 Were Scams", *Cointelegraph: The Future of Money* (www.cointelegraph.com), July 13, 2018.

So, while blockchain and cryptocurrencies remain on the rise, a cautious approach is recommended. That being said, the asset class is developing quickly. For example, while ETFs are not yet available, they are in the works. In addition, the CFA Institute has added these topics as part of an emerging technology and FinTech section of the CFA curriculum, and a number of investment banks have launched Bitcoin trading desks or have commissioned dedicated teams to research the field. The Chicago Mercantile Exchange (CME) began offering Bitcoin Futures in 2017, and Ethereum Futures were launched in May 2018.

We hope the discussion of crypto currencies not only helps fiduciaries consider whether they want to include this particular investment product as a part of a diversified portfolio, but also illustrates the types of issues that can arise with any new investment product that will emerge in the future.

9

Theory Time

The big boon to modern diversification was not just structural in nature with the introduction of the open-end mutual fund; it was also theoretical. In 1952, a young Ph.D. student at the University of Chicago, Harry Markowitz, published a groundbreaking paper, "Portfolio Selection".[1] Markowitz had chosen to apply mathematics to the analysis of the stock market as the topic for his dissertation. While researching the then-current understanding of stock prices, which at the time consisted of the Present Value Model of John Burr Williams, Markowitz realized that the theory lacked an analysis of the impact of risk.

The present value model, in itself, was a positive development in contributing to our understanding of securities prices. Williams was among the first to challenge the "casino" view that economists held of financial markets and asset pricing—where prices are determined largely by expectations and counter-expectations of capital gains. He argued that financial markets are, instead, "markets", properly speaking, and that prices should therefore reflect an asset's intrinsic value. In so doing, he changed the focus from the time series of the market to the underlying components of asset value. Rather than forecasting stock prices directly, Williams emphasized future corporate earnings and dividends, and this view contributed to the "fundamental" basis for investing in securities.

So, Markowitz took a simple concept—"don't put all your eggs in one basket"—and demonstrated how even the addition of a high beta asset (a more volatile, higher-risk stock) could bring down overall portfolio risk through

---

[1] Markowitz, Harry, "Portfolio Selection", *Journal of Finance*, Volume 7, Issue 1, March 1952, pp. 77–91.

© The Author(s) 2019
C. K. Merker, S. W. Peck, *The Trustee Governance Guide*,
https://doi.org/10.1007/978-3-030-21088-5_9

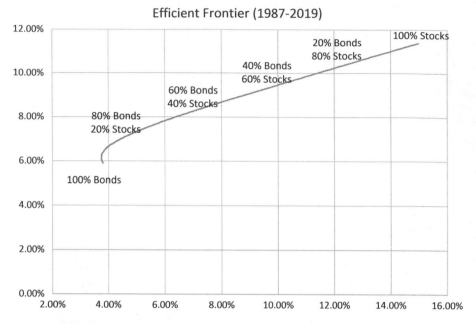

Fig. 9.1   Markowitz's efficient frontier. (Source: Baird)

lower correlation across the asset mix. In retrospect, this was no easy task: How could higher-risk assets reduce overall portfolio risk? In itself, the concept is counterintuitive. The trick was balance within the overall portfolio. The result of this insight led to the development of the efficient frontier in investing (Fig. 9.1).

The efficient frontier is a set of optimal portfolios that offers the highest expected return for a defined level of risk or the lowest risk for a given level of expected return. Portfolios that lie below the efficient frontier are suboptimal because they do not provide enough return for the level of risk. A key finding of the concept was the benefit of diversification resulting from the curvature of the efficient frontier. Optimal portfolios that comprise the efficient frontier tend to have a higher degree of diversification than the suboptimal ones, which are typically less diversified.

One assumption in investing is that a higher degree of risk means a higher potential return. Conversely, investors who take on a lower degree of risk have a lower potential return. According to Markowitz's theory, there is an optimal portfolio that could be designed with a perfect balance between risk and return. The optimal portfolio does not simply include securities with the highest potential returns or low-risk securities. The optimal portfolio aims to balance securities with the greatest potential returns with an acceptable degree of risk or securities with the lowest degree of risk for a given level of potential return.

The point selected on the line by the investor depends on the investor's **risk preference**. Construction of that point on the line depends on a process known as **portfolio optimization**, and is an everyday method of modern portfolio theory (MPT) in today's industry.

Now, the one thing that Markowitz did not capture in his initial work was the effect that time had on a portfolio. While certain investors might view a stock that has fallen in value by 50% over a short period of time as quite risky (i.e., it has a high beta), others might view the investment as extremely safe, offering an almost guaranteed return. Perhaps the stock trades well below the cash on its books and the company is likely to generate cash going forward. This latter group of investors might even view volatility as a positive, creating buying opportunities at various points.

On the other hand, a stock that in the past has climbed slowly and steadily for a long time and has a relatively low beta might sell at an astronomical multiple to revenue or earnings. A risk-averse, beta-focused investor is happy to add this stock to his diversified portfolio, while demanding relatively small expected upside, because of the stock's consistent track record and low volatility. But a fundamentally minded investor might consider the stock a high-risk investment, even in a diversified portfolio, due to its valuation. So, by this argument, there is a tradeoff between risk and return, but volatility and return should not necessarily have this same relationship.

This is where time, as a factor, is also an essential consideration and should inform the investor as to the proper diversification, especially since volatility itself changes over time. To take our example of the overvalued, but low volatility stock, versus the undervalued, but high volatility stock, over time the short-term noise of these two very different assets should dissipate, and the prices of each conform to their long-term fundamental value.

It is important to consider the effect that time has on stocks and bonds. Since 1926 there has never been a ten-year period with a negative return in stocks, and only a handful of five-year periods. While 30 years is a long time in anyone's life—think Keynes' famous dictum "in the long run we are all dead"—for a foundation, endowment, or a pension plan effectively operating in perpetuity that is not unusually long at all.

The other reason time—or the holding period—is such a critical consideration is because of the impact cash flow needs should have on the allocation decision. Because of the highly volatile nature of stocks in the short run, it is important we not subject our assets to the risk of a drawdown at the time we need to raise cash from the portfolio. Therefore, we should factor in the amounts, and timing we need to draw, and build our low-risk, bond position from there.

A rule of thumb is to hold two to three times the amount of annual draw in bonds and cash in determining the percentage amount for "low risk" assets. This is dependent on both the financial flexibility of the organization (i.e., are we able to reduce grants in a year when earnings are less, or negative?) and, of course, the holding period of the portfolio (i.e., in perpetuity, invested for a future capital project in the next three to five years).

Practitioner Focus: Return Targeting

The practical application of theory, combined with goal setting, is an important function of the board. How much do we need and when? Making sure there are enough resources for the organization to continue operating is first in line, right after determining the mission for the organization. An unusual case of a Boys and Girls Club organization in Wisconsin illustrates this point. The organization had allowed its financial resources to drain without any action by the board or senior staff to the point of near bankruptcy. It had cut services during that period of time in reaction to its funding situation, but why or how the organization allowed itself to get down to the last $2000 in its bank account before reaching out to major supporters and contributors remains a mystery.

The community in this case rallied to its cause in this moment of crisis, recognizing the important value of keeping kids off the streets and on the right track in a community that was seeing a rising illicit drug market in its own backyard. And while the board saw a shake-up and the fundraising director was put out on the street, the executive director, who admittedly was good with programming, and therefore valued for this area of expertise, was not held accountable for this situation. This is difficult to understand. Organizations cannot function without financial resources, and that responsibility flows through to fundraising, treasury, and investment management. The board must oversee the end result: fiscal responsibility, and if they do not see results, take proper corrective action. The staff must be engaged and manage these functions effectively.

The organization must also not maintain focus on only one thing alone. Another example makes this point. A private college for many years had been running in the black, and had thereby built up significant reserves, and then one day lost its largest, revenue-generating program to a third party. While the board had been exceptionally good about keeping tabs on the investments, inexplicably it was in the dark on this catastrophic loss to its operation. It was not until the turnover of its president, VP of finance, and the controller, three

Table 9.1 Intermediate-term
capital market assumptions

Asset class	Capital market assumption (%)
Equities	7.8
Fixed income	2.3
Alternatives	12
Inflation	2.5

Source: Baird

years later, with annual fiscal deficits now mounting—and the outlook not particularly good for the school—that the board woke up to this significant structural problem and began to take some corrective measures.

So, to remain fiscally sound, most nonprofit boards must keep sight on three levers: spending, fundraising, and investments. For investments, return targeting is nothing more than goal-setting, and then lining up the allocation policy to support it.

To illustrate this process, let us imagine for a moment that you are responsible for the finances for a university with a $20 million endowment. You use that endowment to help offset annual operating expenses not covered by tuition and grants. Your goal is for that endowment to last for a very long time; in fact, you have a fiduciary obligation to donors to maintain principal across what are known as restricted funds, and so for the purposes of this example let us imagine that 100% of this endowment is donor-restricted. So, you recognize that you can only pull so much out of it each year to maintain principal.

Your investment consultant has indicated that you can rely on the following **capital markets assumptions** to help establish your return targets. First, what is a capital market assumption? These are return expectations over a time period and are used to inform asset allocation decisions. Intermediate-term assumptions are typically over a less than ten-year time period, and long-term are for beyond ten years. For intermediate-term planning, we will rely on a less than ten-year assumption in Table 9.1. By the way, investment consultants serve a similar role for public pension plans, foundations, and other types of trusts.

Now, we turn to determining our return target. Your current approved spending rate is in line with other university and college averages for an endowment of this size, so approximately 4%, or $800,000 per year.[2] On top of your spending rate, you must include a factor for investment expense, for which you will assume all-in a 1% fee that covers the consultant advisory, investment product, and custodial costs, and a factor for inflation. Some

---

[2] Source: NACUBO (National Association of College and University Business Officers).

foundations also incorporate an internal administrative fee to cover staffing costs.

Spending rate	4%
Inflation rate	2.5%
Investment expense	1%
Return target	**7.5%**

The inflation factor is critically important to preserving the purchasing power of the portfolio over time. To illustrate: at a 2.5% rate of inflation to purchase one dollar of goods this year, you will need $1.03 next year, $1.05 the following year, and so on. Thus, you must ensure that your portfolio net of cash flow and expenses is maintaining the line on inflation at a 2.5% growth rate. In our example, a 100% allocation to fixed income, even assuming no withdrawals from the portfolio, would put us 0.2% in arrears each year on inflation.

Once the return target is set, and working with an investment consultant, the organization can essentially then "back-in" to the appropriate, minimum variance, allocation based on the capital markets assumptions above. This can be an iterative process as well for each pool of investments (i.e., endowment, reserves, pension, etc.). This approach to asset allocation allows the organization to set reasonable goals, ensure enough cash flow, and balance risk with return. It should be revisited regularly, however, as capital market assumptions will change, as will the internal needs of the organization. This can be a useful tool for reviewing not only goals, but also helpful in forming allocation guidelines. A review with the investment committee or board should take place at least once per year as part of an annual review of the investment policy statement.

10

Over-Diversification

The old saying "Too much of a good thing…", so it is with diversification. The question is, how much is too much? Peter Lynch, in his book *One Up On Wall Street*, coined the term "diworsification" to describe a company-specific problem: companies investing in areas that were noncore businesses "to diversify" the risk of those businesses. As he, and many others, successfully argued, this approach of the 1970s and 1980s conglomerate just made for inefficient companies. They questioned why companies should diversify their investments, when shareholders and investors can do it themselves by diversifying their own portfolios.

The logic holds, but a problem emerges when the portfolio is chopped up, so much so, that it too has become "diworsified". That is a good place for us to begin, with the question: why don't investors simply hold the market portfolio? And by market, we mean virtually a piece of every asset in the entire world. The first reason you do not is because you have now become the owner of the best- and worst-performing assets in equal measure. This is a sure-fire way toward mediocre returns in the portfolio. As one example of this, Fig. 10.1 shows an optimized US/international portfolio versus the MSCI All World Index over a 20-year investment period. Note the significant difference in performance over time.

The second reason is that the benefits of diversification come from asset classes blended in different proportions. This explains why, despite the fact that US mid cap was the best-performing equity asset class over the past 40 years, an investor would still opt to add other asset classes: risk reduction and return enhancement. Lower correlations between assets will add to the return over time: Less swings in the portfolio and smoother return performance

© The Author(s) 2019
C. K. Merker, S. W. Peck, *The Trustee Governance Guide*,
https://doi.org/10.1007/978-3-030-21088-5_10

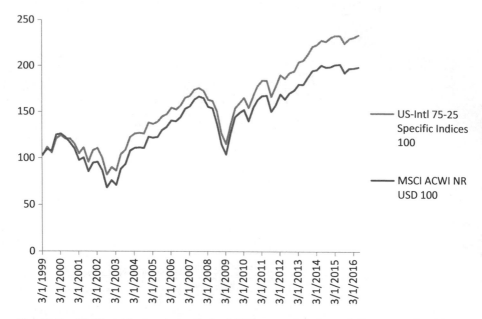

Fig. 10.1 All World Index vs. optimized US/international portfolio—growth of $100. (US/International 75–25 is 40% S&P 500, 10% Russell 1000 Value, 15% Russell Mid Cap, 10% Russell 2000, 20% MSCI EAFE, and 5% MSCI EM. Graph represents the growth of 100 since 1/1/1999 (earliest common inception date). Return and standard deviation are calculated from 1/1/1999 through June 30, 2016. Source: Morningstar Direct)

Table 10.1 Long-term equity market performance, 1979–2015

	Return	Standard deviation
Large cap	11.7	15.5
Mid cap	13.2	16.7
Small cap	11.4	19.5
International	8.7	17.2

Morningstar Direct. Index performance according to the following published indices: Large Cap (S&P 500), Mid Cap (Russell MidCap), Small Cap (Russell 2000), International (MSCI EAFE)

lead to better results. Compounding of smoother return streams drive returns higher over the long run. See Table 10.1 for long-term annualized return performance of various equity market segments.

A perfect example is the owning of both large cap value and large cap growth stocks in the portfolio. Over a long period of time, the last 30 years in fact, the return has been almost identical. But there have been periods where one has significantly outperformed the other over different market cycles. It is in such periods when one group of stock takes off and the other lags that

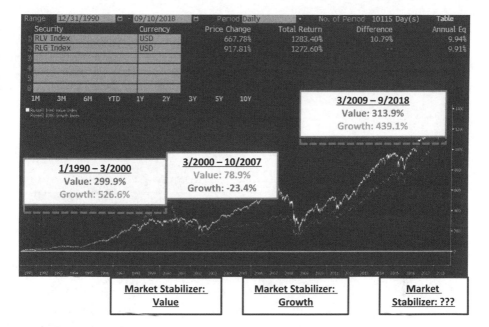

Fig. 10.2 Large cap value and growth—1990–2018. (Bloomberg)

having both in the portfolio has provided a measure of support. Figure 10.2 compares the two indexes. In the 1997–2000 period, growth bubbles up and crashes during the dot-com boom, while value maintains support. In the 2005–2007 period, value rises, particularly due to expansion in the banking sector, and then crashes along with the housing market, and growth at the time provides the ballast, and so forth.

In this period of low interest rates, and dissipating interest in value-oriented dividend payers, and growing interest in growth stocks (no pun intended), particularly in the technology sector, it is uncertain what will provide the ballast in the future. The important thing is that an investor has exposure to both over the long run.

So, not only do boards need to right size portfolio exposures and not needlessly own too many various holdings either globally or through broad indexes, but should also avoid doubling up on too many investment vehicles. What this means is that boards may have the right allocation, but could still have a problem.

The first issue is with indexes. It is not uncommon for a fund to own the S&P 500 multiple ways in a portfolio. The problem with owning an index such as the S&P, especially multiple times, is that the board has now exposed the portfolio to market weights, which means much of the fund's exposure may be tied to the fortunes of fewer than ten companies. What is ironic about

Table 10.2 Top ten
holdings of the S&P
500 by percentage

Company	Percentage of portfolio (%)
Apple Inc	4.33
Microsoft Corp.	3.50
Berkshire Hathaway Inc. B	1.71
JPMorgan Chase & Co	1.62
Facebook Inc. A	1.60
Johnson & Johnson	1.53
Alphabet Inc Class C	1.44
Exxon Mobil Corp	1.44
Alphabet Inc. A	1.43
Total	**18.60**

Source: Morningstar, as of August 31, 2018

this is that where a board thought they were diversified, they are now actually overconcentrated, and in the case of Google (Alphabet) they literally own it twice, in both the A and C shares (See Table 10.2).

Despite the fact that the fund holds 500 names through the index, nearly 20% of the investment is in nine stocks. Keep in mind that the S&P 500 is a market-weighted index, so that as a company grows and outperforms, the index automatically adjusts to buy more of that one stock. Ultimately, the index becomes top heavy to the largest names by market capitalization as we see in its current state. The board in effect is buying high and selling low by definition all the time, as the poorest performing companies in a given period are also reduced.

What happens when these names become overvalued, and the market sells off? The index will take the biggest hit, because these names stand to lose the most ground as they mean revert to—or overshoot—their fundamental value. This is why many have called for more active management during choppy markets, a topic we will cover in more depth in the next section.

Similarly, a bond index is often market cap weighted to the largest issues. This situation, as it relates to debt, is potentially even more perverse in the sense that as an organization issues more and more debt, they become a larger component of the index, so that you have potentially the most indebted issuers among the largest names in the index. Take, for example, the FTSE World Government Bond Index. Japan, one of the largest issuers in the world, is also arguably the most indebted nation in the world. At 20% of the index, it is the second-highest weighting in the index.[1] How well can this index perform over the long run with one of the largest components at a zero rate of interest?[2]

---

[1] Source: Blackrock, as of Jan. 24, 2018.

[2] While the Japanese ten year had been at negative interest rates for years, it has recently climbed back above zero, and as of July 2018, was at 0.83%. In that month, the Bank of Japan had shifted its monetary policy (e.g., yield curve control) to target 0% through bond purchases (quantitative easing).

The second issue could be with the number of managers in the portfolio. Most boards add multiple managers to a portfolio to diversify risk across managers. If having two managers in a sector is better than one, then shouldn't three be better, or even four? If boards add managers with different styles even within a similar group of stocks, their process of ownership and investment will vary enough from each other that, so long as the board is investing in managers that offer a degree of skill in outperforming certain areas of the market, then multiple managers may drive better returns and, again, smooth volatility. However, the inclusion of additional managers, will eventually dilute this positive effect as the asset class begins to look more and more like broader index for the reference group of investments.

At this stage, we understand the reason not to simply buy the global portfolio, and own every stock in the universe. We have also taken the additional steps of analyzing the proportions of small cap, large cap, mid cap, and international, and determined how much of each to own and in exacting proportions. We have even considered the number of managers to hire in each sleeve. Now, why don't we make this easy, and just go out and buy the indexes in each of these subclasses?

At some point it in this book it was inevitable we would have to enter the waters of the Active versus Passive debate, and so this is a good segue into the next imperative, to "Be Disciplined and Control Costs".

Practitioner Focus: Why Overcomplicate Things?

The question must be at some point asked: how complicated do we need to get with this stuff? In investing, this is truly a philosophical question, as much as it is a practical one. The industry, like any other, caters to any and every taste, and has an impressive capacity to churn out product. If an investor is not careful, they will easily fall into the trap of owning too many of the wrong things.

Let us provide an example of this capacity to create product. Chris was at an investment conference and attended a session on the topic of "Factor-Based Investing". What is factor-based investing, you may ask.

Investopedia defines factor-based investing as "a strategy that chooses securities on attributes that are associated with higher returns".[3] Factors include macroeconomic factors and style factors. The former may cover broad risks across asset classes, while the latter aims to explain returns and risks within

---

[3] https://www.investopedia.com/terms/f/factor-investing.asp

asset classes. Some common macroeconomic factors include credit, inflation, and liquidity, whereas style factors embrace style (e.g., value, growth and momentum, just to name a few). You may also hear it referred to as smart-beta or strategic beta. It is essentially a rules-based trading program within a lower-cost investment fund.

At the concept level this all sounds reasonable: Investors want to understand the factors that may influence the returns in the portfolio, minimize risk, and maximize return. A basic level understanding of asset classes will help promote this, but this is where things get complicated very quickly. During the session the asset manager could not be pinned down to what factors were most consequential, and then proceeded to show the audience the approximately 200 factor-based investing products their firm offered. In stark contrast, a portfolio we would typically construct may be, on the outside of the range, composed of just under 30 different investment products, and this would also include alternative investments across private equity, real estate, and reinsurance, with relatively low turnover of investments.[4] We would not know where to begin with 200 products, let alone understand the factor-based models for each. And this is just from one firm. In the marketplace, there are now thousands of such factor-based products.

It is not surprising the asset manager could not be pinned down on which factors matter. Consider that academic research has produced papers on over 300 factors, and that number is growing. At the end of 2014, Campbell Harvey, professor of finance at Duke University's Fuqua School of Business, reported that there were 316 supposed factors covered in top journals and working papers, with new ones being discovered at an accelerating pace—about 40 a year.[5]

For a factor to be impactful, it must be persistent. And the academic research on this is inconclusive. So, if an investor cannot with absolute certainty narrow down the factors, how will an investor select an investment product from what is on offer under this method? Also, let us try a thought experiment: What happens if a factor is identified as the real deal, but then every investor in the market also knows this and responds by allocating their portfolio in the same manner? All that capital chasing that single factor is

---

[4] Benjamin Graham recommended holding 10–30 positions. In today's world that would be considered a highly concentrated portfolio of a single manager. A properly diversified portfolio in today's world may contain exposure to a couple thousand underlying holdings, which is not beyond what you would expect when you consider the full measure of all publicly traded securities and private ones, too, both domestic and international.

[5] Harvey, Campbell R. and Liu, Yan and Zhu, Caroline, "…and the Cross-Section of Expected Returns", February 3, 2015.

likely to change the profit opportunity with respect to that factor. While there may have been a premium associated with investing under that factor, it will likely have completely dissipated after the market has discovered it. Such is the problem with arbitrage, a word often associated with factor-based investing.[6] If there is a 20-dollar bill lying on the sidewalk, how long before someone comes along to pick it up and that bill is gone?

How did the portfolio manager address this issue of factors changing and not persisting? By throwing out another highbrow concept: that of "regime change". This is a fancy way of saying that economic conditions may change. Things like growth rates, interest rates, recessions, and expansions will come and go. So, what to do to as a board? Change out that fund! Get rid of those dirty funds, and replace them with the new shiny ones. Now this sounds a lot like chasing returns, "chasing the hot dot"—buying high and selling low.

How about hedge funds? If you pay "2 and 20", will the fund get long-term abnormal returns (returns above market).[7] Like anything, a hedge fund, which simply put, is an unregulated private investment vehicle, there are few good ones, and then a lot of sub-par offerings. The inherent problem with hedge funds, because they are unregulated, is that they are not particularly transparent about how they earn their returns. Also, the survivorship in this segment is a problem. On average about 800 to 1000 fund open and close each year or about 10%.[8] The returns in hedge funds, as a collective, over the past decade have not been particularly good either, and you will hear this often mentioned. However, that is in comparison to the stock market, which during the same period went in only one direction—up.

Still, the combination of costs, lack of transparency, and inherent risk of whether a chosen product will be open next year renders the asset class down on our list of desirables. The ones that are particularly good are hard to get into, and more often than not closed. The method of investing is also highly variable; is it a long-short, global macro, distressed debt, hedged equity, and so on?

The other thing to keep in mind is that every asset class has this problem. In equity, it could be complicated, factor-based products as we just discussed above. In fixed income, it could be the collateralized debt obligiations (CDOs)

---

[6] Arbitrage is the simultaneous purchase and sale of an asset to profit from an imbalance in the price. It is a trade that profits by exploiting the price differences of identical or similar financial instruments on different markets or in different forms. Arbitrage exists as a result of market inefficiencies and would therefore not exist if all markets were perfectly efficient.

[7] "2 and 20" refers to the typical fee structure of a hedge fund; 2% for the management fee and 20% of the profits.

[8] Source: Bloomberg.

that were particularly popular in the run-up to the housing market crash in 2008, and were comprised of securitized mortgages built out in "tranches". Most of these products ended up being worthless, but were alluring because they offered higher yields at what seemed to be relative safety. In commodities, it could be structured products, or "equity linked notes" that can be both heavily fee-ed and very illiquid, in many cases, only transactable with the one firm that "manufactured" them. And the list goes on.

When people talk about the threat from robo-advisors or artificial intelligence, at least for the individuals providing advice to organizations or individuals, we don't worry. Just sorting through all this flotsam and jetsam is enough to keep those who operate with a measure of integrity and clear-headedness employed. And for those who say "Just index it", as we will discuss in the next section, our rejoinder is "Which one?" In US mid cap alone there are close to 60 different indexes with 200 related products.[9] What criteria will an investor employ to sort through all that? Here a professional can add much more value.

So at the end of the day, how complicated do we need to make this exercise? The short answer: complicated enough, but not overly so. Our research has shown that a diversified portfolio of equity, fixed income, and what we consider direct alternatives, such as a private equity and private real estate, offer the best combination of returns, risk, transparency, tax, and cost control. In our experience, the more complicated the portfolio, the higher the fees, and the greater the turnover; and then the results are less transparency in the investments and more lackluster returns.

---

[9] Morningstar Direct.

Part IV

The Fourth Imperative: *Be Disciplined and Control Costs*

11

The Active Versus Passive Debate

In 2018, Vanguard group passed the $5 trillion mark in assets under management, closing in on BlackRock, the largest with $6 trillion. It was also the fastest-growing manager. Question: How does the largest index fund manager get this big and add $368 billion in a single year?[1] Answer: investors' insatiable desire for cheap, index investing.

The Active versus Passive debate has been raging since the 1970s, and lately the Passive side has been winning, and winning big, with now nearly half of all US equities in some form of index fund.[2] A market that has done nothing but gone straight up since the global financial crisis in 2008 has helped. It all started with the invention of the index fund, the First Index Investment Trust, on December 31, 1975, by Jack Bogle and Vanguard Group. Around the same time, Charles Ellis made waves with his arguments against active investing with the publication of "The Loser's Game" in the July/August 1975 edition of the CFA Institute's *Financial Analysts Journal*.

The argument for passive investing is admittedly compelling in the sense that the fees for active managers can automatically detract from the performance of the fund, and therefore the "alpha" or outperformance of the fund must not only exceed a given benchmark, but a benchmark net of the fee. From there the "passives" simply point to the performance track record of managers, showing that many fail to beat the market, or at least beat it consistently.

---

[1] Flood, Chris, "Vanguard retains title as world's fastest-growing asset manager", *Financial Times*, Jan. 4, 2018.

[2] Merker, Christopher, "Investing: Past, Present and Future", *CFA Enterprising Investor*, April 25, 2018.

© The Author(s) 2019
C. K. Merker, S. W. Peck, *The Trustee Governance Guide*,
https://doi.org/10.1007/978-3-030-21088-5_11

From where did this argument emerge? What are the theoretical underpinnings to it? Since when did beating the market become the mantra? For that we have to turn once again to academic research, and in this case turn the clock back a bit more to the late 1960s, and the development of the Efficient Market Hypothesis (EMH).

The EMH is a theory in financial economics that states that asset prices fully reflect all available information. A direct implication is that it is impossible to "beat the market" consistently on a risk-adjusted basis since market prices should only react to new information. Further, this new information can be either positive or negative.

The theory was developed by Eugene Fama, a Nobel Prize winner from the University of Chicago, one of many, who argued that stocks always trade at their fair value, making it impossible for investors to either purchase undervalued stocks or sell stocks for inflated prices.[3] As such, it should be impossible to outperform the overall market through expert stock selection or market timing, and the only way an investor can possibly obtain higher returns is by chance or by purchasing riskier investments. His 2012 study with Kenneth French supported this view, showing that the distribution of abnormal returns of US mutual funds is very similar to what would be expected if no fund managers had any skill—a necessary condition for the EMH to hold.

There are three variants of the hypothesis: "weak", "semi-strong", and "strong" form. The **weak form** of the EMH claims that prices on traded assets (e.g., stocks, bonds, or property) already reflect all past publicly available information. The **semi-strong form** of the EMH claims both that prices reflect all publicly available information and that prices instantly change to reflect new public information. The **strong form** of the EMH additionally claims that prices instantly reflect even hidden "insider" information.

There is no quantitative measure of market efficiency, and so, testing the idea is difficult. So-called event studies provide some of the best evidence, but they are open to other interpretations. Event studies look at large samples of a type of information announcement, for example, earnings, CEO change, and so on, and measure the average market reaction to the announcement. With few exceptions, these studies support the notion that markets react to information immediately and completely. Yet, critics have blamed the belief in rational markets for much of the late-2000s financial crisis. See Chap. 4 for a thorough discussion of behavioral finance, a theory that has developed as a counter-argument to investor rationality and market efficiency.

---

[3] Fama was awarded the Nobel for his work in 2013.

In response, proponents of the hypothesis have stated that market efficiency does not mean not having any uncertainty about the future; that market efficiency is a simplification of the world, which may not always hold true; and that the market is "practically efficient" for investment purposes for most investors.

Fama demonstrated that the notion of market efficiency could not be rejected without an accompanying rejection of the model of market equilibrium (e.g., the price setting mechanism). This concept, known as the **joint hypothesis problem**, has vexed researchers ever since. Market efficiency denotes how information is factored into price, and Fama emphasizes that the hypothesis of market efficiency must be tested in the context of expected returns. Think back to our discussion in the last section on **factor-based investing**. The joint hypothesis problem states that when a model yields a predicted return significantly different from the actual return, one can never be certain if there exists an imperfection in the model or if the market itself is inefficient. Researchers can only modify their models by adding different factors to eliminate any anomalies, in the hopes of fully explaining the return within the model.

Thus, there is another type of information under the EMH. This is talent or private information. Investors that have above-average skill in analyzing public information such as financial statements have this private information which they can use to find stocks that are either undervalued or overvalued by the market. Investors with superior stock picking talents are akin to insiders with nonpublic information. Active managers purport to have such skills and the ability to generate returns that are higher than the risk-adjusted returns predicted by the model, known as "alpha". They can charge higher fees because they generate alpha.

Alpha is also the anomaly in the modeling test, and thus functions as a signal to the model maker whether it can perfectly predict returns by the factors in the model.[4] As long as there is an alpha in the model, neither the conclusion of a flawed model nor market inefficiency can be drawn according to the Joint Hypothesis. Hence, there remains uncertainty as to whether active management has a role to play in the fund's portfolio. We provide evidence in the next chapter to help resolve this uncertainty.

---

[4] Alpha comes from the estimate of an additional term in the model estimation. Statistics has a long tradition of Greek symbols in estimating equations which has leading to terms such as alpha and beta in investments.

12

Active Versus Passive: The Evidence

The Efficient Markets Hypothesis predicts that in markets where information is readily available and widely known, there are less likely to be profitable opportunities for stock pickers or active managers. In these markets, it makes more sense to use passive investments and forgo the higher fees of active managers. Correspondingly, in markets where there is both less quantity and quality of information, there will be profitable opportunities for talented stock pickers to buy and sell mis-priced stocks. In these markets, active managers can be well worth their fees.

As part of Chris' Ph.D. program, he decided to examine the Active vs. Passive debate himself with an empirical study. He approached his research with the understanding, as he had seen in his professional career over the years, that certain segments of the market are highly efficient, especially for large corporate stocks, and should be indexed as cheaply as possible, while others are highly inefficient, such as the municipal bond market.

In that study, we pulled 20 and 30 years of data on thousands of mutual funds across several subclasses of equity, including large cap core, large cap value, large cap growth, small cap, and international. We limited our data set to funds that had sufficiently long track records. The objective was to understand whether fund managers could outperform within their segments, and if so, what was (1) the likelihood of that outperformance and (2) the magnitude of that outperformance.

The reason behind looking at likelihood was if the probability was low, then why bother, just index it. Likewise, even if the probability of outperformance was decent, but the magnitude of outperformance was minimal, again, why bother, just index it.

© The Author(s) 2019
C. K. Merker, S. W. Peck, *The Trustee Governance Guide*,
https://doi.org/10.1007/978-3-030-21088-5_12

We, of course, came at this like any other good research project, with a hypothesis. That hypothesis was that certain areas of the market may in fact be very efficient. Large cap value, for example, has stocks that are very well covered in the market by sell side analysts and the mainstream media. With such ample information in the market, the thinking is that this market segment should be highly efficient and difficult for any manager, even one with skill, to outperform.

Conversely, a segment of the market that could be highly varied and disparate, such as international, with its tens of thousands of stocks from dozens of countries could be quite inefficient, with less information, or at least more "gating" of that information. Information is either not easily accessible, or alternatively, there can be simply too much information around too many stocks to efficiently process it.

Likewise, small cap US equity is comprised of many, many smaller names, not particularly well-known companies, nor covered particularly well within the market. Here, these subclasses within the market could be much less efficient and provide an opportunity for a manager with skill to realize persistent outperformance over time, that persistent performance being driven by a Graham and Dodd–type of fundamental research process.[1]

To derive any conclusions, that persistent outperformance in our analysis needed to be statistically significant over time, and not random. Here is what we found. Fig. 12.1 shows the mean excess returns for the top-tier managers in the sample.[2] And indeed, there are excess returns available in the market from this group. Now the next question is: was this excess return consistent?

Figure 12.2 shows the frequency (or percentage) of outperforming managers by asset class segment. These managers statistically outperformed their

---

[1] In 1934, David Dodd and Benjamin Graham, Warren Buffet's mentor, wrote *Security Analysis*, which came to be known as the foundational book on value investing. Graham and Dodd came up with a method for valuing stocks, primarily looking for deeply depressed prices. They sought out stocks that had a high earnings-to-price ratio, a low P/E based on its history, a high dividend yield, a price below its book and net current asset value. In addition, they wanted to see total debt less than book value, a current ratio greater than two, earnings growth of at least 7% for the past ten years, and no more than a 5% decline in earnings in more than two of those ten years. According to their research, these screening methods were predicators for consistent outperformance over time.

[2] This was for 92 managers with 240 monthly observations from January 1994 to December 2013. To reduce our four segments to a manageable sample, in large cap growth and value we took only those managers that on a cumulative return-basis outperformed the average of the overall peer group. In international and small cap, we used all managers whose return record was available across the entire sample period. We broke each group into two segments:

1. Tier 1 – managers who outperformed the index on a cumulative basis.
2. Tier 2 – managers who underperformed the index on cumulative basis.

In large cap core, we had an even longer time frame available of 30 years, or 360 observations.

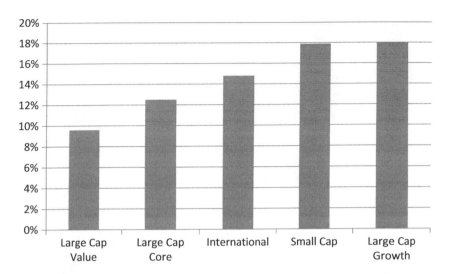

Fig. 12.1 Top-tier managers, mean excess annual returns, 1994–2013

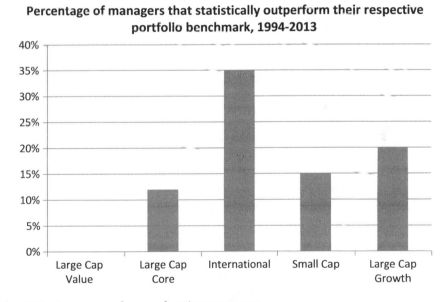

Fig. 12.2 Frequency of outperforming managers

respective portfolio benchmark over the time period. This answers the question of how likely it is that managers can consistently outperform in their respective segment. As we anticipated, large value offers absolutely no opportunity, and this was borne out in the analysis. Any outperformance by a manager was simply by chance. However, in the other segments, particularly

Frequency of outperformance

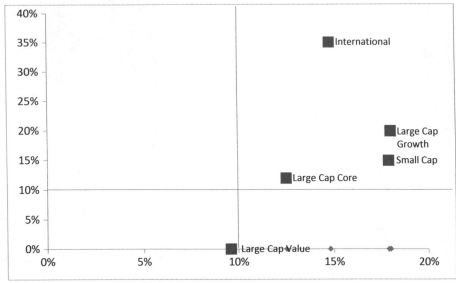

Magnitude of outperformance

Fig. 12.3 Quadrant summary

international, small cap, and large cap growth, there was plenty of opportunity to find a manager to provide net-of-fee outperformance. Large cap core was a bit of a push, and indeed, particularly over the past decade, it has been very difficult for a manager to outperform the S&P 500.

Figure 12.3 plots these asset classes according to both scales, and a clear picture emerges. Anything in the upper right quadrant should be invested with an active manager, or ideally, with a group of active managers (but not too many—recall the lessons in Chap. 9).

This, of course, is just looking at stock managers. If we had looked at bond managers, the results would, more than likely, have been even more striking. Without going into a lot of depth on why this would be the case, suffice it to say that there are many features of the bond market that make this area of the financial markets particularly inefficient. First, bonds trade the old-fashioned way, "over the counter", or OTC. What does OTC mean? It means I call you to see if you want to buy from me or sell to me a bond. Many firms over the years have made runs at creating an exchange for bond trading, but to no avail. The market is too big, too illiquid, too fragmented, and frankly, too unregulated, particularly in the case of municipal bonds, to avail itself to this model. In fact, academic studies on bond market efficiency are virtually nonexistent. Plain and simple, it is hard for researchers to collect the data and analyze it. If it is that hard just looking at the data, imagine how hard it is for the people trading every day in the market.

How bonds get priced is the second feature of market inefficiency. A transaction price is negotiated between two parties, as we mentioned, OTC. However, any bond that is priced on an investor's statement may not have been traded for a long time, and we do not mean just the investor's holding, any of the same issue in the market. Yet, the investor will still see a price. That price is brought to you by one of three pricing services that provide "matrix pricing". Because many bonds trade infrequently, one bond's price is often based on a similar issue (credit quality, type of issuer, maturity, etc.) that traded more recently. So, the price on your bond may not even be your bond's actual price, but from another bond, and so the carrying value of your bond could actually vary significantly from what it actually gets marked at when sold or purchased in the market.

Therefore, a hybrid approach is recommended utilizing both active and passive investments. Where active is used, the selection process and discipline must be in place. Goyal and Wahal in a 2008 landmark study found that institutional investors are not particularly effective on the timing of hiring and firing investment managers. What they found in examining thousands of hire/fire decisions by over 3000 pension plans over a ten-year period is that on average plan sponsors (pension funds) have no timing ability. The transition to a new manager, in itself, can be a costly process as it poses both opportunity and friction costs that range from 1% to 2% of the asset value. While they found the behavior of funds not irrational in their motivations, the results themselves on average, after costs, are no better than if no change had been made at all.

Their findings are consistent with what Chris has seen in his professional experience, and frankly, has occasionally fallen victim to. Sarah saw the same issue again and again when serving on the pension board. For anyone watching a manager underperform for some time, the tendency is to do something about it. The only thought for most is "We need to do something to fix this!" And, oh, by the way, managers frequently underperform, so that urge comes around often. S&P Dow Jones conducted a study covering the years 2000–2016 and found that for managers that outperformed in one year, they were just as likely to underperform in the next year.[3] This does not mean you abandon a manager for a single year of underperformance, but you do need to fight the tendency to do just that. This is where investment discipline is especially important.

---

[3] Anderson, Tom, "Active fund managers rarely beat their benchmarks year after year", CNBC, February 27, 2017.

13

Cost Savings and What Really Matters

In the department of "not seeing the forest for the trees", something very odd happened a number of years ago to our investment culture despite good research on the topic. In 1986, Gary P. Brinson, L. Randolph Hood, and Gilbert L. Beebower (BHB) published a paper in the *Financial Analyst Journal* entitled "Determinants of Portfolio Performance". They sought to explain the effect of asset allocation policy on pension plan returns, a topic that had largely been unexplored up to that point. BHB asserted that asset allocation is the primary determinant of a portfolio's return variability, with security selection and market timing (together, active management) playing minor roles. A linear time-series regression yielded an average R-squared of 93.6%, leading BHB to conclude that asset allocation explained the variation in a portfolio's quarterly returns more than 90% of the time.

They went on in 1991 to update the study and confirmed the same results. In the parlance of today, the results went viral, and found their way into the marketing pitches of most investment advisors. Others in the industry and the academe have since gone on and found similar results.

So, why is this? Follow us through this string of logic. If we tell you that one course of action will drive more than 90% of the result, and two other courses of action combined will drive less than 10% of the result, where would you spend most of your time? The answer should be obvious. The question then is, why do boards spend so much time on manager selection and so little time on asset allocation? The proliferation of investment products is one clear indication. The idea underpinning a wide-ranging investment product market is that if I try "this" versus "that" I will get a better result, so I better have a lot of "this" and "that" to look at.

© The Author(s) 2019
C. K. Merker, S. W. Peck, *The Trustee Governance Guide*,
https://doi.org/10.1007/978-3-030-21088-5_13

A 2014 Mercer survey of European pensions found that nearly 70% of boards take responsibility for manager selection. So, why would a board want to spend any time on manager selection, especially given, from that same survey, that nearly 80% are only conducting investment reviews once per year or less?[1]

OK, if a board on average is spending most of what little time it has on manager review and selection, then are they spending less time on asset allocation? One way to gauge that is to examine the percentage of plans applying LDI (liability-driven investing), also known as liability matching. The idea is that if boards look out into the future and understand what and when they will need to fund beneficiary obligations, then they can line up investments to match those payouts on a time-horizon basis. The idea extends into liability immunization and so forth and can be an effective way of ensuring there is enough funding long-term, and that the fund's investments are not invested too conservatively (i.e., too heavy a weighting in bonds) at least in the short run. If a plan is using LDI, then they are definitely spending time on asset allocation. But from that same survey, only 29% of plans are engaged in applying this technique.

If boards know that asset allocation is so important, then that is where trustees should be spending their time. This is in addition to the 30% that delegate manager selection to an investment consultant. For an effective board that has limited time to spend on investments, this combination is the best approach balancing time, priority, and impact.

Cost Control

Now let us talk about cost control. Industry surveys in recent years have consistently highlighted investment expense as a top five issue. For example, from a recent McKinsey survey: *Across the industry, many pension funds are under intense scrutiny by boards and stakeholders to cut costs.*[2] The survey, depending on the size of the pension system, cited that between 2% and 42% of defined benefit pension plans were under pressure to cut costs.

---

[1] Asset Allocation Survey: European Institutional Marketplace Overview 2014, Mercer, http://info.mercer.com/rs/mercer/images/13080-IC%202014%20European%20Asset%20Allocation%20survey%20report_FIN_SEC.PDF

[2] http://www.statestreet.com/content/dam/statestreet/documents/Articles/pensionswithpurpose/Pensions_With_Purpose_Report.pdf

And yet, no survey (or study to our knowledge) to date has asked the question, how much does cost actually matter for the plan? There is a presumption that it must matter a lot, and so the question is asked this way frequently.

An emphasis on cost savings is generally a positive and not a negative for any organization. But, in the case of organizations responsible for investments, and to bring it back to governance, cost-consciousness can eclipse more important considerations like investment objectives, purpose, allocation, cash-flow needs, and risk. In a 2017 article that appeared in *Enterprising Investor*, Chris asked the question out loud whether investment expense had, in fact, become a proxy for good governance.[3]

As discussed earlier in this section, with this emphasis on cost control, investors have flocked into index products. With that has come, especially recently, a race to near zero in the cost of these funds, or the expense ratio. If investors can meet the minimums, they can now invest in a large-cap core index product for 1.5 basis points (bps). That trumps the cheapest Vanguard fund (Vanguard 500), which is trading at a relatively heavy 9 bps. Chris is also aware of a separately managed account index that is actually free if the investor agrees to let the index manager lend out their securities.

Our study, of course, focused on the governance and effectiveness of large institutional investors. We constructed a model of Fiduciary Effectiveness™ to understand the performance drivers of these larger institutions. We looked at the effect on investment returns and funding ratios of several factors, including investment expenses. We found:

> *For the control variables . . . with the exception of investment expenses, we had no particular expectation of signs. In the case of investment expenses, it was surprising on a couple of levels: 1) we expected that this would be a detractor to returns, and the opposite relationship was indicated in the estimation, and 2) the estimated coefficient was not statistically significant. The reason why this was a surprising result is because the industry has become obsessed with investment expenses over the past several years, which has fed into a debate over 'active' (higher-cost, research-driven, and actively managed investments) versus 'passive' (lower cost, index-defined) investments, and in this case we found no such relationship to investment returns.*

Investment costs don't matter? How could that be?

If you pay less for something, does that not imply you keep more for yourself? Not if you gave up something else in the process. For many investors, what is "given up" is performance. And not "active" performance necessarily,

[3] https://blogs.cfainstitute.org/investor/2017/10/09/investment-expense-as-a-proxy-for-good-governance/

but governance-based performance, or what we refer to as structured group investor behavior.

It could be any number of decisions made by pension trustees: market timing, allocation decisions, or manager selection and termination, for example. But when the governance leading to these decisions is weak, so follows the discipline and the performance. According to our research, hundreds of basis points in performance are lost. So, you initially saved 25 bps, but gave up 200 bps relative to your better-performing peers?

Let's examine the data.

The graph below tells the story (Fig. 13.1). It compares the average performance of the top and bottom five public pension plans based on five-year investment returns. *Though the bottom five saved 25% on investment costs on average, they returned 80% less.* The Fiduciary Effectiveness Quotient™ (FEQ) score is also included to gauge the difference in the governance index. Consistent with our other findings, the bottom five scored 30% below the top on average.

So, instead of focusing on enhancing the performance metric, net of costs, the scrutiny has been directed at the investment cost side of the ledger. Why have investment expenses become such a focus? Because costs are concrete numbers that change very little over time; they provide a measure everybody can sink their teeth into. Performance numbers are the opposite: They are speculative, uncertain, and out in the future. It is human nature to want to control what we can control. We can make decisions about and act on

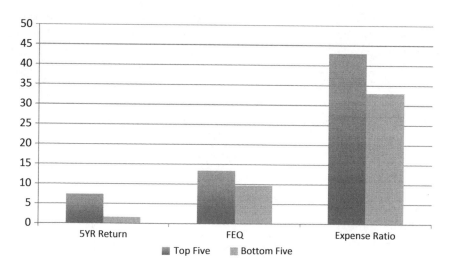

Fig. 13.1 Average of top five and bottom five public pension plans as ranked by five-year investment returns

investment expenses and feel good about it. This is how controlling investment expenses became a proxy for good governance.

Regardless of where you stand on the active versus passive debate, the overwhelming evidence shows that investors in general, but specifically the boards and organizations they serve, have not been effective. From our study, 60% of public fund performance was at or below average—mostly below. The Dalbar study of individual investor behavior consistently shows the problem is not confined to institutions.

Cost is, no doubt, an important consideration, but it is not the only consideration; when it swamps others that can be a problem. Boards with limited time need to focus on what counts. If they only had time to think about the asset allocation issue, that would be time well spent. Manager selection and cost control, while important things for a board to cover, can also get in the way of consistent long-term strategy and discipline if that is all they think about. The data, as we saw, and as they say in academic research, supports this conclusion.

Practitioner Focus: Fee and Expense Reports: What to Ask Your Consultant for on an Annual Basis

Determining what you are paying for investments may not be as straightforward as you might expect. As a trustee, knowing what you are paying and having an oversight on costs is part of one's fiduciary duty. One example of not keeping oversight is the New York City pension system, which was heavily criticized in the media for paying out $2.5 billion in manager fees (mostly hedge funds) over a ten-year period, during which it earned a nearly 0% rate of return, net of fees.[4] While nobody was sued or went to jail over this, it did generate a good deal of unwanted publicity for the trustees charged with oversight of the plan.

Fees and expenses can come from several sources. There are first the product costs associated with the individual investments. These are the fees paid to the investment managers. In a separate account, the fee is charged by the custodian from the account. There may also be commissions from the buying and selling of individual securities (transaction costs). If it is a mutual fund or an exchange-traded fund, the fee and any related transaction costs are charged

---

[4] McGeehan, Patrick, "Wall Street Fees Wipe Out $2.5 Billion in New York City Pension Gains", *The New York Times*, April 8, 2015.

from within the fund, and reported as an expense ratio, which simply states the annual fee as a percentage of the assets contained within the fund. Fees can range on the low end from a few basis points (a basis point = 0.01%) for index funds to, on the upper end, "2 and 20" fees for hedge funds (2% management fee, and 20% of the earnings, or "carry", above a specified hurdle rate, or minimum rate of return).

The investment advisor or consultant providing advice and related services (manager research, reporting, etc.) will also collect an advisory fee. Like an investment manager, this is typically determined as a percentage of the assets under advisement or it may also be an annual flat dollar amount.

The third source of fees is related to the custodian. The custodian, which could be a broker-dealer, bank, or trust company, may charge a fee for safe-keeping of the assets. This cost, again based on the value of the overall assets, can range from a few basis points on up. There may also be banking-related fees, account service fees, fees for movement of money, such as wire fees, and so on. For pension plans, there will be an additional service fees related to the Third Party Administrator, or TPA, for record keeping and the actuary for actuarial estimates and reporting for current and future liabilities vis-à-vis plan assets.

All these fees can—and should be reported—at least on an annual basis. While not a requirement, a good consultant will provide an annual fee summary that breaks out advisory fees, management fees, and custody fees. The regulators also now require annual disclosure of trading and commissions costs. Trustees should also request a summary of banking and other transaction costs. When going out to the market to conduct an Request for Proposal (RFP) process, it is important to request this information from service providers being considered for the mandate. Providing them a template to fill in with estimated costs can provide a framework of making costs comparable across firms competing for the work. This is important because firms report fees differently, and not necessarily comprehensively. So, giving firms a template to fill in makes certain that the data you are getting back is comparable.

Finally, a documented, annual review of fees and expenses is an important step to keeping oversight on the issue. What you should find is that a good advisor will bring about cost reductions year over year through ongoing negotiation with outside managers. If you are dealing with an advisor that is marketing its own products, be careful that an inherent conflict of interest exists and is more than likely inhibiting such fee reductions from taking place.

Part V

The Fifth Imperative: *Be Impactful*

14

Farewell to Uncle Milt

The unblinking and hard-nosed theory of shareholder value and the idea that a corporation is nothing more than a "profit-maximizing unit" found no greater support than from the great monetarist and libertarian, Milton Friedman. He was once quoted famously as saying:

> *There is one and only one social responsibility of business – to use its resources and engage in activities designed to increase its profits so long as it stays within the rules of the game, which is to say, engages in open and free competition without deception or fraud.*[1]

Times have changed, and that view has shifted in recent years, even though socially responsible investing (SRI) has been around for as long as portfolio diversification, if not longer. However, its widespread and transformative effect on investing culture did not begin to take hold until the better part of the last decade.

One can point to very early religious restrictions around investment that go back to biblical times. Ethical investing was mandated by Jewish law, and investment activities, like anything else, were intended to correct human-driven imbalances to God's Creation. Several 100 years later the Quran, thought to have been written in the 7th century, banned usury, which extended to the forbidding of all interest payments, and ruled out investments in alcohol, pork, gambling, armaments, gold, and silver (other than for spot cash, not as an investment).

---

[1] Friedman, Milton, *Capitalism and Freedom*, Phoenix Books, 1982.

© The Author(s) 2019
C. K. Merker, S. W. Peck, *The Trustee Governance Guide*,
https://doi.org/10.1007/978-3-030-21088-5_14

In the US, SRI began with the Methodists in the 18th century. Investments were not permitted to have anything to do with the slave trade, smuggling, and conspicuous consumption, and this additionally applied to companies manufacturing liquor or tobacco products or promoting gambling. The Methodists were followed in 1898 by the Quakers, who forbid investments in slavery and war, and then by a group in Boston who founded the first publicly offered, socially responsible mutual fund, the Pioneer Fund, in 1928. Most of these early strategies applied screens to eliminate "sin" industries. And for the next 60 years, SRI remained the niche domain of religious endowments and foundations.

Then, starting in the early 1990s, things began to shift. We can point to three seminal documents that over the next two decades helped articulate and drive the transformation from more narrow SRI forms of investing to broader ESG (environmental, social, and governance) investing. **The Cadbury Report** in 1992 set out recommendations on how to arrange company boards and accounting systems to mitigate corporate governance risks and failures. The **UN Principles of Responsible Investing (UNPRI)**, established in 2005, laid out guidelines for responsible investing and invited the formal participation of asset managers and asset owners. And in 2014, David Swensen's **"Letter on Climate Change"** called on investment managers broadly to consider the carbon impact of their investments. Swensen has been the Chief Investment Officer (CIO) at the Yale University endowment for the past two decades, and is credited with being one of the best CIOs in the world given his outstanding return record. When he made that formal request, many listened.

Even into the early years of the new millennium, however, the major part of the investment market still accepted the historical assumption that ethically directed investments were by their nature likely to reduce financial return. Philanthropy was certainly not known for being a profitable area of activity, and Milton Friedman provided a widely accepted basis that the costs for corporations, who spent time worried about anything beyond earning a return to their stockholders, would exceed the benefits. However, this assumption has since been fundamentally challenged.

The main reason why Friedman's earlier view has been successfully challenged is because ESG is not about philanthropy, but about risk management. As long-time believers in human freedom and the wisdom of the market, we would be the first to agree with Friedman's perspective that the domain of effective philanthropy, is not only best served by individuals, but it is the most appropriate form of expression of values by individuals. One of Friedman's basic tenets is that corporations are not people. Friedman also often said that companies with too much cash should payout to shareholders to let them make better portfolio investment choices, and he said similar things about philanthropy. But managers seeking to manage risks and profitability in the long run should also be concerned about ESG factors and not just leave these concerns to the philanthropists.

So, why is the integration of ESG factors into investment analysis important for the reduction of risk? First, we need only look back at the corporate governance failures of the late 1990s and later 2000s in the financial sector to understand how crucial good corporate governance is to avoiding financial disaster. The Enrons, WorldComs, AIGs and Lehman Bros. of the world stand out as embodiments of what can go wrong on a massive scale as a direct result of corporate governance failures.

Research began examining the links between corporate governance, social responsibility, and financial performance. One source of that examination leveraged the work of Robert Levering and Milton Moskowitz, who had developed and maintained the **Fortune 100 Best Companies to Work For** list for over two decades.[2] Their research concerned how these companies were managed, what the stakeholder relationships were, and how the employees were treated. They successfully demonstrated that improving corporate governance procedures and social impacts across the workforce did not damage financial performance, but in contrast, maximized productivity, ensured corporate efficiency, and led to the sourcing and utilizing of superior management talents.

Where Friedman provided the academic support for the argument that the integration of ESG-type factors into financial practice would reduce financial performance, numerous reports began to appear in the early years of the century that provided research that supported arguments to the contrary. In 2006, Oxford University's Michael Barnett and New York University's Robert Salomon published an influential study that concluded that the two sides of the argument might even be complementary—they propounded a curvilinear relationship between social responsibility and financial performance.

Furthermore, they found that both methods of factor and nonfactor integration could maximize financial performance of an investment portfolio. The only route likely to damage performance was partial integration. So, if one were going about ESG investing, one needed to fully commit to it.[3]

---

[2] Moskowitz, Milton and Levering, Robert, "The best employers in the U.S. say their greatest tool is culture" *Fortune*, March 5, 2015.

[3] Barnett, Michael and Salomon, Robert, "Beyond dichotomy: the curvilinear relationship between social responsibility and financial performance", *Strategic Management Journal*, V. 27, No. 11, pp. 1101–1122, November, 2006.

Table 14.1 Top risks to global development

Likelihood	Impact
Extreme weather events	Weapons of mass destruction
Natural disasters	Extreme weather events
Cyber attacks	Natural disasters
Data fraud or theft	Failure of climate change mitigation or adaptation
Failure of climate change mitigation or adaptation	Water crisis

In 2011, Alex Edmans, a finance professor at Wharton, followed up with a paper in the *Journal of Financial Economics*.[4] In that paper, Edmans showed that the **100 Best Companies to Work For** outperformed their peers in terms of stock returns by 2–3% a year over 1984–2009, and delivered earnings that systematically exceeded analyst expectations.

Concomitantly, the risks to business from climate change have come into focus for investors and insurers. Last year Chris attended an ESG conference, and one of the panelists, an analyst from MSCI, indicated that, based on their forecasts, climate change alone could negatively impact the value of over 40% of publicly traded stocks over the next 10 years. Data in Table 14.1 summarizes the top five risks by likelihood and impact to global development according to a 2018 World Economic Forum report, which does an annual review of these risks, produced in conjunction with Marsh & McLennan and Zurich Re.[5]

Water noted among one of the top five risks in 2018, has been a concern for global business for some time now. As early as 2014, most global businesses polled said they already face severe water scarcity risks for their operations, according to a report by CDP, a nonprofit group that provides environmental information on businesses and government entities to investors.[6] This risk can impact revenue, decrease shareholder value, and force substantial changes in strategy. The survey also noted that insufficient water resources could simply constrain growth.

In addition, environmental management practices have spurred bottom line improvement for business. Many companies are now finding that lowering the carbon footprint, reducing waste, and becoming more sustainable can

---

[4] Edmans, Alex, Does the stock market fully value intangibles? Employee satisfaction and equity prices, Journal of Financial Economics 101 (2011) pp. 621–640.

[5] World Economic Forum, "The Global Risks Report", 2018 https://www.weforum.org/reports/the-global-risks-report-2018

[6] https://www.cnbc.com/2014/11/07/water-scarcity-an-immediate-threat-to-global-businesses-survey.html

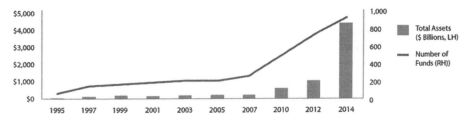

Fig. 14.1 US investment funds incorporating ESG factors. (Baird)

result in energy, water, and waste management savings. It can also increase profit through efficiency or productivity gains.

Besides the large investment companies and banks taking an interest in matters of ESG, an array of investment companies specifically dealing with responsible investment and ESG-based portfolios began to spring up throughout the financial world. In fact, in some respects the opposite problem has now occurred with too many embracing ESG without enough regard to the rigor required to make ESG effective. Wall Street has a penchant for fashion, and when something comes into fashion, it is not uncommon to see a wave of products hit the market, often at the expense of quality (product proliferation). We may be there already. There are now 221 mutual funds and ETFs that invest based on ESG criteria, up from 130 in 2012.[7]

In May 2017, Chris published an article "The Stampede into ESG" in *Enterprising Investor* that highlighted the sudden shift among asset managers into this arena that focused on data from one chart (Fig. 14.1).[8]

In that article Chris observed,

The move (in the U.S.) from $1 trillion in 2012 to over $4 trillion just two years later surprised me — a 300% change as the number of funds grew from around 650 to roughly 800. The most recent data from 2016, which is not shown in the chart, indicates nearly $9 trillion in total assets.

The question that struck me when I saw all this: Did all of the asset managers that are now factoring ESG into their investment process shift all $4 trillion in assets the day they signed up with the PRI?

The answer, of course, is no. Nothing changed. Not really, anyway. While the move into ESG investing demonstrates greater consciousness on the part of investment managers, the factors themselves are 'soft' in their application. As Christopher Scott Peck, Hal Brill, and Michael Kramer observed in The Resilient Investor: '. . . we

---

[7] Loder, Asjylyn, "Painstaking Progress for Fund that Aim to Do Good", *Wall Street Journal*, March 21, 2019.

[8] Merker, Christopher K., "The Stampede into ESG", *CFA Enterprising Investor*, May 29, 2017.

recognize that the softer ESG 'considerations' approach, while a step in the right direction, is less socially and environmentally impactful than SRI's traditionally more active approach of designing portfolios and mutual funds to screen out the worst actors and seek out companies charting beneficial new directions'.

The problem for investors is how to first define their specific objectives and then audit or enforce those objectives under their given mandate. Eliminating tobacco stocks from a portfolio is straightforward enough. Controlling the carbon footprint of a portfolio is a different matter altogether. Holding asset managers accountable to a given set of goals and standards is key.

The potential is there though. A 2015 comprehensive meta-study of the academic research conducted over the last 30 years provided additional long-term support for the ESG focus. In "ESG and Financial Performance: Aggregated Evidence from More Than 2000 Empirical Studies", Gunnar Friede, Timo Busch, and Alexander Bassen applied a meta-analysis of ESG studies since 1979 and concluded that 90% show statistical evidence of a relationship between ESG factors and positive financial results.[9]

Many in the investment industry believe the development of ESG factors as considerations in investment analysis to be inevitable. The evidence toward a relationship between consideration for ESG issues and financial performance is becoming greater, and the combination of fiduciary duty and a wide recognition of the necessity of the sustainability of investments in the long term has meant that environmental, social, and corporate governance concerns are now becoming increasingly important in the investment market.

There has been uncertainty and debate as to what to call the inclusion of intangible factors relating to the sustainability and ethical impact of investments (terminology). Names have ranged from the early use of buzz words such as "green" and "eco", to the wide array of possible descriptions for the types of investment analysis—"responsible investment", "socially responsible investment" (SRI), "ethical", "extra-financial", "long horizon investment" (LHI), "enhanced business", "corporate health", "nontraditional", and others. But the predominance of the term ESG has now become widely accepted. You will also often hear the term "non-GAAP" to differentiate this set of factors from traditional financial metrics. A survey of 350 global investment professionals conducted by AXA Investment Managers and AQ Research in 2008 concluded most professionals preferred the term ESG to describe such data.

---

[9] Gunnar Friede, Timo Busch & Alexander Bassen (2015) "ESG and financial performance: aggregated evidence from more than 2000 empirical studies", *Journal of Sustainable Finance & Investment.*

The rise and growing ubiquity of ESG is not the product of any single innovation but rather represents a reinvention of the entire industry. Consider this: Roughly 100 data analytics firms, among them Sustainalytics and MSCI, have sprung up in recent years to gather environmental, social, and governance (ESG) data on corporations and other investments.

In the meantime, thousands of investment managers have embraced ESG for fear of being left behind. What the true impact the widespread adoption of these practices will have is yet to be determined. But the trickle of new ESG- or impact-related investment products, including mutual funds and ETFs, has now become a flood.

Practitioner Section: Doesn't ESG Investing Pose a Conflict with Fiduciary Duty?

The short answer is no. Not so long as returns are equal to or in excess of what they would have been without ESG integration, all other things being equal. What about the return record? Can we substantiate this? Yes and no. It depends on the methodology. ESG integration return performance is as varied as that of manager performance, as is the case with all investing. One recent study we can point to, certainly the most comprehensive to date, looked at over 2000 ESG studies since the early 1970s and found that 90% of the studies demonstrated a significant relationship between ESG and corporate financial performance.

In looking at the fiduciary relationship, the United Nations Environment Programme Finance Initiative (UNEP FI) in 2005 commissioned a report from the international law firm Freshfields Bruckhaus Deringer on the interpretation of the law with respect to investors and ESG issues. The Freshfields report concluded that not only was it permissible for investment companies to integrate ESG issues into investment analysis, but it was arguably part of their fiduciary duty to do so. In 2014, the Law Commission (England and Wales) confirmed that there was no bar on pension trustees and others from taking account of ESG factors when making investment decisions.

Interest in ESG and sustainable investing also runs strong for plan participants according to a Natixis' 2016 Survey of Defined Contribution Plan Participants. In fact, more than six in ten participants agreed they would be more likely to contribute or increase their contributions to their retirement plan if they knew their investments were also doing social good. In January 2016, the PRI, UNEP FI, and The Generation Foundation launched a 3-year project to end the debate on whether fiduciary duty is a legitimate barrier to the integration of environmental, social, and governance issues in investment practice and decision-making.

This follows the publication in September 2015 of "Fiduciary Duty in the 21st Century" by the PRI, UNEP FI, UNEP Inquiry, and UN Global Compact. The report concluded that "failing to consider all long-term investment value drivers, including ESG issues, is a failure of fiduciary duty". It also acknowledged that despite significant progress, many investors have yet to fully integrate ESG issues into their investment decision-making processes.

In January 2019, CFA Institute came out with the following updated policy statement on ESG in support of fiduciary duty by stating[10]:

> *A key point in the ESG Statement is the duty of CFA® charterholders to factor all material information, including key ESG elements, into investment analysis, unless doing so would be contrary to client wishes. The ESG Statement notes that such factoring is consistent with an investment manager's fiduciary duty.*

However, it also produced this additional caveat in the statement:

> *The ESG Statement addresses growing concerns about products that managers are loosely marketing as ESG strategies to investors. It supports the development of a proper taxonomy that requires full disclosure and validation of ESG strategy claims. In addition, the ESG Statement recognizes that not all investment strategies and managers employ active, fundamental analysis. In the case of index products, for example, managers should alert their clients as to the extent and the means by which ESG factors are featured in these types of passive investment products.*

---

[10] https://cfainstitute.org/advocacy/policy-positions/positions-on-environmental-social-governance-integration

15

ESG Challenges

We have heard mentioned that there are two kinds of people involved in the ESG movement: those that are hard-nosed finance people, along with a few academics, who really know how to "push the numbers", and another group who represent the "feel good" group. Based on what we have reviewed in the literature and what is out there in practice, we need more of the former and less of the latter, because this movement has some issues. The good news is that we think in general we are on the right track, and there is enough professionalism, momentum, and industry structure behind this now to keep things moving in the right direction.

When we began teaching sustainable finance at Marquette University more than a decade ago, environmental, social, and governance (ESG) investing and socially responsible investing (SRI) were still backwaters. A lot, as we talked about in the previous chapter, has changed even over the recent years. However, the increasing adoption and application of these types of investing criteria conceal some underlying challenges. Despite the rapid growth of ESG funds across several measures, we still see four main obstacles to continuing emergence of ESG investing. Below we outline these challenges, and chart the progress toward potential solutions.

Defining Standards and Terminology A survey conducted in 2017 by State Street Global Advisors found that over half of those institutional investors already implementing some form of ESG strategy in their portfolios were struggling with clarity around standards and terminology.[1] That shows

---

[1] "Performing for the Future: ESG's Place in Investment Portfolios. Today and Tomorrow", State Street Global Advisors ESG Institutional Survey, 2018 https://www.ssga.com/investment-topics/environmental-social-governance/2018/04/esg-institutional-investor-survey.pdf

© The Author(s) 2019
C. K. Merker, S. W. Peck, *The Trustee Governance Guide*,
https://doi.org/10.1007/978-3-030-21088-5_15

considerable confusion on the subject. MSCI scores ConocoPhillips an A, the third-highest rating available. That is, comparatively speaking, a relatively strong ESG rating. So good that two of the largest asset managers in the world both hold ConocoPhillips in their ESG funds.[2] To include or not to include? Are we avoiding the oil sector altogether or not? Maybe the strong "non-GAAP"-related performance and transparency demonstrated by energy companies should be embraced? Or maybe not. This issue creates a real conundrum for investors, and there are, of course, many less extreme, if no less challenging, examples to untangle in this context.

Another criticism targets the ESG ratings firms themselves. Their ratings are inconsistent due to significant differences in data collection, analysis, and reporting. Indeed, ratings are rarely the same, or even similar, for a given company. And, as noted, there are a lot of competing data providers.[3] The empirical argument on ESG yielding better risk-adjusted performance is untenable if we cannot point to consistent standards. If our interpretation of the data leads us to use one rating and not another and that trade makes our portfolio worse off, what then? As we discussed in the last section, trustees have a fiduciary obligation to their clients and beneficiaries in almost all cases to match or outperform, and ESG's most important claim is that doing good will drive better returns. That argument is weakened by inconsistent ratings. As James Mackintosh from the *Wall Street Journal* observed, Warren Buffett's Berkshire Hathaway was ranked dead last in the S&P 500 by one ratings firm and in the middle of the pack by another.[4] That is simply too much of a discrepancy.

We should strive for greater consistency, as we see with bond ratings, and for ratings differences among the ratings agencies to become more the exception than the norm. But that consistency needs to be driven by something other than human judgment. Rather, it needs to be tied to both financial and impact results.

Standards and reporting are catching up through the good work of such organizations as the Sustainable Accounting Standards Board (SASB). The SASB's complete set of codified standards came out in 2018. The launch of products such as the Morningstar Sustainability Rating in late 2016 and ISS-Ethix were likewise positive developments for fund analysis.

[2] Kauflin, Jeff, "Do-Good Investors: Watch Out For What These Funds Hold", Forbes, December 6, 2017 https://www.forbes.com/sites/jeffkauflin/2017/12/06/portfolio-placebos/#5618a7564c04

[3] Douglas, Elyse et al., "Responsible Investing: Guide to ESG Data Providers and Relevant Trends", *Journal of Environmental Investing*, Vol. 8 No. 1, 2017 https://cbey.yale.edu/sites/default/files/Responsible%20Investing%20-%20Guide%20to%20ESG%20Data%20Providers%20and%20Relevant%20Trends.pdf

[4] Mackintosh, James, "If You Want to Do Good, Expect to Do Badly", *Wall Street Journal*, June 28, 2018.

How ESG expresses values needs to be better understood, and the gray area made less gray in relation to SRI principles. Are we investing for better performance, impact, or both? In the long run, wouldn't impact lead to better performance? What makes one ESG manager different from another? Better performance, impact or both? Standardization of disclosure and reporting to investors will help.

ESG Adoption Awareness and understanding of ESG and its role need to improve. We also need to clarify how ESG differs from SRI and even impact investing. Institutional investors are having conversations on these issues, and adoption rates are brisk of late, but a few others are jumping in, especially among retail investors.

Demand for ESG methods should help mitigate risk and drive higher returns on the asset management side of the business. As asset managers increase their understanding of ESG as a core investment process, the notion of an ESG product as distinct from other active or indexed products should start to wither away. ESG will just become the way investing is done and will theoretically be applied to all manner of investing.

At some point, no one will ask whether a security is ESG or not. They may inquire what values are expressed or what constraints are in place, as we see today with SRI. Asset managers are clearly not waiting for investors to establish standards. Rather, perhaps too many are claiming to be ESG managers without any standards of practice attached to that.

The Quality of ESG Information We need more and better issuer disclosures as well as more insightful data. Too much of the available ESG information is of poor quality. There are lots of people and organizations working on this problem—the Global Reporting Initiative (GRI), Governance and Accountability Institute (GAI), and SASB, among them—and it should eventually sort itself out.

However, information overload is a Big Data problem that requires better quantitative methods. An investment manager, client, or investment board looking at a report may only be interested in a single index measure. That measure needs to be well-researched and robust to be effective. It is time for ESG to become more of a science and less of an art. This should help address the consistency problem as well.

ESG in Other Investment Markets As the *Wall Street Journal* reported in 2017, private markets have eclipsed the public markets for the last six years in a row when it comes to new issuances.

We have all heard about the incredible shrinking equity market, wherein the number of publicly traded companies is about half what it was two decades ago. The question is, how does all this ESG work find its way into an area of investing that is overtaking the more traditional forms?

ESG has a natural home in the public markets, which already have ongoing disclosure requirements. Unfortunately, these requirements are why many companies no longer want to remain public.

But what about other areas, say, municipal bonds? One of the constraints on the growth of ESG municipal exchange-traded funds (ETFs) is the lack of data available to the exchanges. Governments need to be held to the same standards as public companies, especially in light of the rapid growth in green bonds, recent tax legislation around Opportunity Zones, and the emergence of social impact bonds (SIBs), not to mention the controversies around such major defaults as in Detroit and Puerto Rico, financial and social distress in Dallas, Illinois, and Connecticut, and water quality in Flint, Michigan.

Practitioner Focus: What Exactly Is the Difference Between SRI and ESG?

The confusion around terminology is symptomatic of the main underlying ambiguity between socially responsible investing and ESG investing. Let us discuss for a moment why there might be some ambiguity around this.

First off, investors have different values. Not only do investors have different values, but the intensity with which they hold these values also varies. For example, Chris had one investor come to him recently, and wanted him to construct a portfolio that focused on reduced carbon impact, human rights, diversity issues, and no weapons. Not because she believed this would reduce risk or earn higher returns. For her, this was simply exercising principles that were important to her. And she was a strict adherent across all four areas. Chris and his colleagues had to find funds that hit the bell on all four criteria. This, make no mistake, was an SRI portfolio, and not an ESG portfolio, even though he used "ESG" funds.

What made this an SRI portfolio, and not an ESG portfolio? The expression of values. ESG in its purest form is risk reduction and return enhancement. If reducing carbon impact means lower costs and higher earnings, or better water management leads to sustained revenue, then it belongs in the portfolio. How an investor feels about environmental impacts or satisfying their concerns about social equity does not enter in the picture. Once it does then the ESG focus has morphed into an expression of an SRI viewpoint.

Characteristics of SRI

Investments are driven first by ethical values, or by nonfinancial objectives. Organizations prohibit investment in certain companies or industries depending on the investor's criteria. For example, some community-based organizations prohibit investment in hand-gun manufacturers.

SRI is typically more narrowly defined by the investor. For example, an organization may divest the portfolio of the top 200 fossil fuel companies. The SRI screens themselves are different for different investors. Some organizations impose religious or ethical screens that restrict alcohol, gaming, or fetal tissue research companies. Tobacco screens are applied often times by health-related organizations. Sudan, South Africa, and weapons manufacturers have been the focus of some divestment campaigns for a range of investors. The key point is that different organizations have different priorities, so SRI criteria are not universal but very organization-specific.

There are other forms. **Divestment** was noted above, and is similar to boycotting. Such coordinated investor movements have been historically successful in South Africa in bringing about the end to apartheid in the 1980s, and more recently in the Sudan around concerns of genocide across the region in the 2000s. Today's divestment campaigns are targeting Big Oil on the basis of concerns around climate change.

Investor activism is another form, and the Interfaith Council on Corporate Responsibility (https://www.iccr.org) is one such group that coordinates corporate engagement with boards of companies to drive social change. Activists will initiate proxy votes or fights to bring issues to the fore among shareholders and in the media. Even though most of the time activists do not win their proxy fight, the issues they raise can lead to regulatory changes, such as "say on pay" increased disclosure requirements, or industry changes, such as the lower use of sweat shops in the athletic and footwear industry in the early 2000s.

Impact investments is another broad subcategory, and can involve anything ranging from Opportunity Zone investments, as part of recent US tax reform legislation, to Economically Targeted Investments (ETN) to social and environmental impact bonds. What they have in common is that they are creatures of public policy attempting to leverage investments for social change. Impact bonds have certain defined objectives (i.e., better water quality, reduced recidivism among prisoners) that must be met before the investments pay-off to investors.

Characteristics of ESG

The inclusion of sustainability factors guides investment research to identify companies with higher investment potential. Specific investments are not prohibited, but rather rankings are assigned to ESG factors for a company in any industry. These ESG rankings are used as part of the overall investment research process. Poor rankings do not necessarily exclude a company from investment, but are cause for further evaluation and consideration.

ESG incorporates a broad set of factors to guide security selection. For example, which natural resource companies are less likely to experience catastrophic events because of their environmental and safety practices? ESG is still in development, so the application of these factors will evolve, but the theory is that certain factors have broad applicability to all investment options. For example, good governance, strong shareholder rights, and transparency are positives for investors in any company.

An ESG focus, while risk- and return-based, also can have the desired effects of reinforcing positive impacts across these three dimensions of environmental, social, and governance factors; in other words, a desired focus on sustainability can legitimately—and most often will—follow as a secondary objective for ESG investors.

16

OK, We've Bought In...Now What?

So, let us say for a moment the board has bought in to the fifth imperative, "Be Impactful", and the board now wants to retool your organization's portfolio to start heading down this path. What do you do and what resources are available?

First, the board will need to decide whether you are about sustainability or you have more stringent requirements. Are there certain values, beliefs, or principles held by your organization that need to be expressed in the portfolio?

Chris was recently reviewing a set of values of one religious order, and in it they described concerns about ESG, and sustainability in general, and then they had further restrictions around nuclear power, carbon emissions (energy), weapons, pornography, and contraception. This set of requirements required first an ESG screening of funds using the Morningstar Sustainability Rating (a product provided by Sustainalytics through Morningstar), and then a secondary screening of names that would fall under an SRI restriction using ISS-Ethix, which produced a list of names in the investment portfolio that would violate this set of criteria. The organization established a minimum ESG rating of the broad index, and then Chris and his colleagues worked with them on threshold tolerances for the other set of criteria. If a fund was in excess of 10%, then the fund was removed from the portfolio.

This process, once established, required ongoing quarterly review and reporting. It also required a rewrite to the investment policy statement (see sample below). There may be additional consideration given to how the portfolio and mission of the organization is supporting the UN's Sustainable Development Goals (or SDGs). More information on these goals, organizations, and principles is provided below.

© The Author(s) 2019
C. K. Merker, S. W. Peck, *The Trustee Governance Guide*,
https://doi.org/10.1007/978-3-030-21088-5_16

Industry Resources

Standards Organizations

Standards organizations are important for stating the principles, particularly around sustainability, as well as providing standards around information disclosure to investors and other stakeholders. There are a number that have come to the fore in recent years.

SASB: Sustainability Accounting Standards Board

SASB develops and disseminates industry-specific accounting standards for material sustainability issues for the purposes of integrated reporting. The SASB standards are suitable for disclosure in standard filings (such as Form 10-K and 20-F in the US context) but are broadly applicable and relevant globally for companies looking to report on material environmental, social, and governance (ESG) issues. SASB has developed standards for 88 industries in ten sectors using a multi-stakeholder, transparent process. The standards describe both impacts as well as opportunities for innovation. Taken together, "they characterize a company's positioning with respect to sustainability issues and the potential for long term value creation".[1]

UN PRI: United Nations Principles of Responsible Investing

The United Nations–supported Principles for Responsible Investment (PRI) Initiative is an international network of investors working together to put the six Principles for Responsible Investment into practice. Its goal is to understand the implications of sustainability for investors and support signatories to incorporate these issues into their investment decision-making and ownership practices. In implementing the Principles, signatories contribute to the development of a more sustainable global financial system.

The Principles are voluntary and aspirational. They offer a menu of possible actions for incorporating ESG issues into investment practices across asset classes. Responsible investment is a process that must be tailored to fit each organization's investment strategy, approach, and resources. The Principles are designed to be compatible with the investment styles of large, diversified, institutional investors that operate within a traditional fiduciary framework.

---

[1] See www.sasb.org

The PRI Initiative has quickly become the leading global network for investors to publicly demonstrate their commitment to responsible investment, to collaborate and learn with their peers about the financial and investment implications of ESG issues, and to incorporate these factors into their investment decision-making and ownership practices.[2]

The Six Principles

1. Incorporate ESG issues into investment analysis and decision-making processes.
2. Be active owners and incorporate ESG issues into our ownership policies and practices.
3. Seek appropriate disclosure on ESG issues by the entities in which we invest.
4. Promote acceptance and implementation of the Principles within the investment industry.
5. Work together to enhance our effectiveness in implementing the Principles.
6. Report on our activities and progress towards implementing the Principles.

UN SDGs: United Nations Sustainable Development Goals

The 17 Sustainable Development Goals (SDGs)—part of a wider 2030 Agenda for Sustainable Development—build on the Millennium Development Goals (MDGs). These eight goals were set by the United Nations back in 2000 to eradicate poverty, hunger, illiteracy, and disease.

The MDGs were concrete, specific and measurable, and therefore helped establish some priority areas of focus in international development. But that was also one of their biggest criticisms: by being so targeted, they had left out other, equally important, areas.

Despite the criticism, significant progress has been made over the past 15 years, especially when it comes to the goals of eradicating poverty and improving access to education. That progress, however, has been very uneven, with improvements often concentrated in specific regions and among certain social groups. A 2015 UN assessment of the MDGs found they fell short for many people: "The assessment of progress towards the MDGs has repeatedly shown that the poorest and those disadvantaged because of gender, age, disability or ethnicity are often bypassed".

---

[2] See www.unpri.org

In developing the SDGs—a multi-year process involving civil society, governments, the private sector, and academia—the United Nations sought to take all these failings into account. In response to the accusation that the MDGs were too narrow in focus, the SDGs set out to tackle a whole range of issues, from gender inequality to climate change. The unifying thread throughout the 17 goals and their 169 targets is the commitment to ending poverty: "Eradicating poverty in all its forms and dimensions, including extreme poverty, is the greatest global challenge and an indispensable requirement for sustainable development," notes the agenda's preamble.

With the SDGs, the UN states the following mission on the website: "The Sustainable Development Goals are the blueprint to achieve a better and more sustainable future for all. They address the global challenges we face, including those related to poverty, inequality, climate, environmental degradation, prosperity, and peace and justice. The Goals interconnect and in order to leave no one behind, it is important that we achieve each Goal and target by 2030." See Fig. 16.1 for the 17 goals.[3]

Fig. 16.1 UN's 17 sustainable development goals

---

[3] See https://sustainabledevelopment.un.org/sdgs

United Nations Global Compact

The United Nations Global Compact is a United Nations initiative to encourage businesses worldwide to adopt sustainable and socially responsible policies, and to report on their implementation. The UN Global Compact is a principle-based framework for businesses, stating ten principles in the areas of human rights, labor, the environment, and anti-corruption. Under the Global Compact, companies are brought together with UN agencies, labor groups, and civil society. Cities can join the Global Compact through the Cities Programme.

The UN Global Compact is the world's largest corporate sustainability (corporate social responsibility) initiative with 13,000 corporate participants and other stakeholders over 170 countries with two objectives: "Mainstream the ten principles in business activities around the world" and "Catalyze actions in support of broader UN goals, such as the Millennium Development Goals (MDGs) and Sustainable Development Goals (SDGs)". Moving forward, The UN Global Compact and its signatories are dedicated to supporting progress toward the SDGs.[4]

The Ten Principles

Human Rights

Principle 1: Businesses should support and respect the protection of internationally proclaimed human rights.
Principle 2: Make sure that they are not complicit in human rights abuses.

Labor

Principle 3: Businesses should uphold the freedom of association and the effective recognition of the right to collective bargaining.
Principle 4: The elimination of all forms of forced and compulsory labor.
Principle 5: The effective abolition of child labor.
Principle 6: The elimination of discrimination in respect of employment and occupation.

---

[4] See www.unglobalcompact.org

Environment

Principle 7: Businesses should support a precautionary approach to environmental challenges.

Principle 8: Undertake initiatives to promote greater environmental responsibility.

Principle 9: Encourage the development and diffusion of environmentally friendly technologies.

Anti-Corruption

Principle 10: Businesses should work against corruption in all its forms, including extortion and bribery.

US SIF: The Forum for Sustainable and Responsible Investment

The Forum is the leading voice advancing sustainable, responsible, and impact investing across all asset classes. Its mission is to rapidly shift investment practices toward sustainability, focusing on long-term investment and the generation of positive social and environmental impacts. US SIF members include investment management and advisory firms, mutual fund companies, asset owners, research firms, financial planners and advisors, broker-dealers, community investing organizations, and nonprofit organizations.[5]

Data Providers

Over the last five years, there has been a gold rush mentality in the data and analytics business for supporting ESG. One recent NYU paper estimates that there are over 100 companies serving this market today.[6]

Presently there are primarily four major companies that provide ESG ratings and rankings on mostly publicly held corporations: Sustainalytics, MSCI, ISS, and FTSE-Russell. RobecoSAM is another provider through Bloomberg. The methodologies for assessing an ESG rating vary significantly across the providers. See Table 16.1 for a summary of providers and methodologies.

---

[5] See www.ussif.org

[6] Douglas, Elyse et al., "Responsible Investing: Guide to ESG Data Providers and Relevant Trends", *Journal of Environmental Investing* Vol. 8 No. 1, 2017.

Table 16.1 Which one? ESG data firms and methodologies

ESG data firm	Methodology
Bloomberg ESG data services	120 ESG indicators
Corporate knights global 100	14 key performance indicators
DJSI	Industry specific questionnaire – 80 to 100 questions (annually)
FTSE-Russell	300 indicators, 14 themes, avg. 125 indicators per company
ISS	ISS quality score / ISS-Ethix (ongoing)
MSCI ESG	37 key ESG issues (annually)
RepRisk	28 ESG issues and 45 "hot topics" (daily)
Sustainalytics	70 industry-specific ESG indicators
Thomson Reuters	400 ESG metrics (every 2 weeks)

Each firm is primarily geared to provide ratings on individual securities, but many are working toward a portfolio approach, which is more accessible to investors directly. Morningstar introduced the Morningstar Sustainability Rating in 2016, which provides mutual fund and exchange-traded fund level ratings, and ISS at the time of this writing is working toward investor tools that provide portfolio level measures. It is worth noting that with the exception of some sovereign and corporate bonds, corporate stocks are almost exclusively covered, and this is certainly true on a fund basis. If an investor is interested in getting private corporate information, they will be hard-pressed to find much of anything. ISS does have some coverage, but it extends to mostly "controversy" information, that uses media as its primary source.

Practitioner Focus: Writing an ESG Policy into Your IPS

Putting together an investment policy for responsible investment is a requirement, particularly as it relates to ensuring your fiduciary duty remains intact. Each organization does it a little differently. The Intentional Endowments Network is a good a resource for finding a variety of sample investment policies that range from Stanford University's to University of Edinburgh's.[7]

The Network states that good policies, defined as both effective and broadly supported, share common traits:

---

[7] http://www.intentionalendowments.org/investment_policy_statements

They have articulated their purpose, priorities, and principles and integrated these pillars within their investment policies and decision criteria. One key to arriving at this point is the investment of time. Effective ESG policy creation requires a process of stakeholder engagement that includes education about and exploration of the sustainable investing thesis, field, and opportunity set.

Here is a brief one-page example from the University of Oregon:

Statement of Investment Principles Board of Trustees of the University of University of Oregon Sample IPS

The University of Oregon's investment philosophy is anchored in the following core principle, which is fundamental and constant. Assets controlled by the University must be managed in accordance with this principle, regardless of the ebbs and flows likely to arise due to markets, politics, and personalities.

The primary principle guiding the University's investments is the consideration of financial impact(s) on current and future elements of the university. This manifests itself through investment practices that generate the greatest possible return, subject to an appropriate amount of risk, to support the institution's mission of teaching, research and service. In fulfilling this vision, only advisors and investment managers with appropriate institutional sophistication and an understanding of best practices will be considered. The Board of Trustees maintains ultimate responsibility for monitoring the performance of various pools of university assets and related returns.

Within the context of this primary principle, the University must consider a holistic view of risk that accounts for various factors, which could modify a return/risk objective. These include:

- Maintaining appropriate levels of liquidity for the university's operational needs;
- Mitigating downside financial risks;
- Understanding and appropriately managing reputational risk or legal liability; and,
- Protecting university assets from politically-motivated pressures.

Additionally, academic research supports the practice of incorporating environmental, social, and governance ("ESG") factors with other conventional financial analytical tools when evaluating investment opportunities as these factors may help identify potential opportunities and risks which conventional tools miss. The UO encourages its advisors and managers to include ESG factors in their analytical processes. However, ESG considerations are only one factor in analyses and should not be used as exclusionary screens to eliminate specific entities or sectors from consideration. Relevant ESG factors will vary by industry and should be applied appropriately to help assess both risk and return.

Adopted by the Executive and Audit Committee.

Index[1]

---

[1] Note: Page numbers followed by 'n' refer to notes.

© The Author(s) 2019
C. K. Merker, S. W. Peck, *The Trustee Governance Guide*,
https://doi.org/10.1007/978-3-030-21088-5